Paula—
What do you
say to the woman
who has it all? nati?
Charm, brains...
I pray

Moving On

will go
smoothly, quickly
and, ok, efficiently.
Not that all the "stuff"
has gotten you down, but
just in case it does—
keep smiling
and moving on!
Love—
Julie

Moving On

A Practical Guide to
Downsizing the Family Home
How to Get Rid of the Stuff,
Keep the Memories, Maintain the Family Peace,
and Get on with Your Life

Linda Hetzer & Janet Hulstrand

Illustrations by **DAVID McGRIEVEY**

STEWART, TABORI & CHANG • NEW YORK

Text copyright © 2004 Linda Hetzer and Janet Hulstrand
Illustrations copyright © 2004 David McGrievey/Arts Counsel Inc.

Published in 2004 by
Stewart, Tabori & Chang
A Company of La Martinière Groupe
115 West 18th Street
New York, NY 10011

Export Sales to all countries except Canada, France,
and French-speaking Switzerland:
Thames and Hudson Ltd. · 181A High Holborn
London WC1V 7QX · England

Canadian Distribution:
Canadian Manda Group · One Atlantic Avenue, Suite 105
Toronto, Ontario M6K 3E7 · Canada

Library of Congress Cataloging-in-Publication Data
Hetzer, Linda.
Moving on : a practical guide to downsizing the
family home / by Linda Hetzer and Janet Hulstrand.
p.cm.
ISBN: 1-58479-323-6
1. House Cleaning. I. Hulstrand, Janet. II. Title.
TX324.H48 2004
648'.—dc22   2003065880

DISCLAIMER: The authors are not experts in the fields of law, finance,
medicine, or family counseling. The information offered
in this book does not lessen the need for, nor take the place of, legal,
financial, medical, or any other professional advice.

The authors and the publisher shall have neither liability nor
responsibility to any person or entity with respect to any loss or damage caused,
or alleged to be caused, by the information contained in this book.

The text of this book was composed in Sabon, Gill Sans and Koloss.
Edited by Marisa Bulzone
Designed by Susi Oberhelman
Graphic Production by Kim Tyner

Printed in China by C & C Offest Ltd.

10   9   8   7   6   5   4   3   2   1

FIRST PRINTING

To my parents, Ruth Johnson Hetzer and
Theodore J. Hetzer, who kept family treasures
and told stories about them,
all of which helped bring the past to life.

And to Michael, who is my present.

And to Emily and Elizabeth, who are my future.

L.H.

To the memory of my mother,
Carolyn Powers Hulstrand,
who filled our home with many, many things—
but most of all, with love.

And to my brother, sister, and father—
and all the uncles, aunts, cousins,
nieces, and nephews—who made the experience
of emptying out our house *almost* a pleasure.

And to Steve, Phineas, and Sammy, always and forever.

J.H.

Contents

Introduction

EVERY CHILD KNOWS THAT IT'S MORE FUN taking toys out and playing with them than it is putting them away again when you're done. And many older people (or their middle-aged children) are finding out that it's much more fun building up a home and filling it with beautiful furnishings, wonderful objects, and meaningful memorabilia, than it is trying to figure out what to do with them all when the house has served its purpose and it's time to move on.

When the time comes for you (or your parents) to leave behind your family home—whether it's because of illness, death, or simply changing needs or preferences—play time is over, and it's time to put away the toys. But where do you put them all, and how? In what order do you work? And how can you do it in such a way that family harmony (if it exists) remains intact, and family dysfunction (if it doesn't) is not exacerbated? So that everyone is able to move on to the next stage of life with some sense of positive resolution; with a good deal of poignancy, perhaps, but no bitterness.

We are two adult daughters who have recently had the experience of helping our fathers move out of the houses they had occupied for several decades—the homes we grew up in—and into apartments. Because our fathers had continued to live in their homes for a number of years after our mothers had passed away, we were both able to separate the task of cleaning out the house from mourning the death of a parent. Even so, we found that the job was a challenging one, both physically and emotionally.

There were many reasons for this. One was that both of us come from families of savers. Not only did our parents find it difficult to throw things out, but in both cases our homes had been the repositories for items that had belonged to our parents' parents and grandparents, as well as aunts and uncles who had passed away earlier. Our parents' homes were very full! So the task that fell to us (and the sisters and brothers who were working with us), of sorting and throwing things out, was time-consuming.

It was also a bit problematic, because we knew that among the many things we needed to just get rid of, there were also a lot of meaningful family treasures we wanted to save, for ourselves and for our children. That meant looking at and making decisions about every single thing in those houses, drawer by drawer and item by item. It was, in a word, overwhelming!

At the time, we both wished there had been a guide we could turn to that would give us some idea about the various options for dividing up the household objects, disposing of what no one wanted, and carefully saving family treasures. And as we talked to others who were going through this process it became clear that for most people this is at best a complicated experience. We discovered that we were far from alone in feeling the need for practical information and advice, as well as the comfort gained in hearing other people's stories.

In this book we have put together what we, and the people we talked to, learned in the process of emptying out our family's homes. Along the way, we discovered a wonderful variety of creative, witty, sometimes ingenious solutions to some of the pitfalls families easily fall into even when they enter this process with the best of intentions and are in general agreement on how to proceed.

The good news is that, while this is a big job and it can be overwhelming, with the right approach, enough time, and a little bit of luck, clearing out the family home can also be a positive experience. It can offer wonderful moments of nostalgia, new chances to heal old wounds, and great opportunities for family bonding. We hope that the ideas, strategies, and insights we've collected in these pages will help you and your family use this time to find those moments and make the most of those opportunities.

That is why we wrote this book. We hope it will help you make this experience the best it can be.

LINDA HETZER AND JANET HULSTRAND

Moving On

First Things First

WHEN IS IT TIME TO EMPTY THE house? There are really two answers to this question. The first answer is that it's different for every family; it's very hard to know when to start, and it's even harder to go about actually doing it. The second answer is that the time to start is now! The one piece of advice we heard more than any other as we worked on this book, from almost everyone we spoke to, was "Take your time!" We think this is good advice that can't be overstated for a number of reasons. This is a big job and, as such, the more time you have to devote to it the better off you and your family will be in the long run. This book includes suggestions for steps you can take to begin the process well ahead of time. This will help things go more smoothly and gradually, and can make the final stages less hurried and stressful for everyone involved.

Who is this book for? Well, it's for anyone involved in the process of emptying out a family home, either as the principal or as a family member. You might be a couple preparing to move from your family home into a retirement community; you could be a middle-aged child helping your parents move out of the house you grew up in; you might be going through the house after the death of your parents or another relative. You might even be a middle-aged individual making a move for career or personal reasons, and the home you're moving into is smaller than the one you're moving out of.

If you've picked up this book, it's probably time for you to start thinking about the day when you will have to empty the house. But before you start packing up and throwing things out, let's take a moment to look at the big picture.

PLANNING AHEAD, AND REMEMBERING WHO'S IN CHARGE

One of the most difficult things for families to adjust to as parents age is the subtle, and sometimes not-so-subtle, shifting and altering of roles that takes place. It is natural and right for adult children to help their parents more and more as their parents advance in age, but it is also extremely important for them to continue to respect their parents' autonomy and independence as much as possible. This can be the trickiest of balancing acts, to say the least, and it can be extraordinarily difficult for the children in the family to draw appropriate boundaries and stay within those limits. It's also a constantly evolving process, and what is appropriate this year may no longer be appropriate a year from now. But just because it's hard doesn't mean it can't be done.

Planning ahead is crucial. If you are the parent, it is important for you to realistically address the possibility that you may one day need to move out of your home, and at the very least line up various options for what you will do if that is the case. It will be much easier on both you and your children if you take steps to prepare for your future now, when you are able to do so and have a greater choice of options, than if you leave your children to deal with the consequences of your failure to plan ahead. Many people would prefer to live out the rest of their lives in the homes where they have spent many happy and productive years, but the reality for most people is that at some point the responsibilities of caring for a house and yard are simply too demanding, and the benefits of staying in the family home diminish. And many people, even those who dread taking the step of making such a move, are happy and relieved once they have done it.

It's the funniest thing: I don't miss the house at all. The problems we were having in it were such that I was able to leave it behind with no regrets. We really had happy years in our home. It was not an ostentatious house, but it had a nice big yard that we loved. We had a wonderful watercolor artist take pictures of our house in late spring and winter, and then paint two different scenes of it. They're hanging over our bookcases in our new den, and they bring back good memories.

If you are the child of aging parents, the first thing to remember in dealing with the very big question of when to empty the family home is that whenever possible that decision should be made by the people living in it. You can help move the process forward by initiating discussions, being involved and supportive in the decision making, and helping your parents research various options. But you should try to let your parents be the ones who actually make the decisions about when and where to move.

Can We Talk About It?

Starting a conversation about what will happen when the family home is emptied is not easy. For most people, anything that forces them to think about their mortality is difficult. But it really is the best way to make the transition, whenever it comes, easier for everyone involved.

TALKING WITH YOUR KIDS

▶ **Discuss your estate plan with your kids.** Having a plan does *not* mean you're about to die, and it may or may not include drawing up a will. Estate planning should be a lifelong process, one that your attorney, tax advisors, and accountant can help you keep up to date. It will be easier for your heirs to take care of whatever needs to be dealt with when you're gone if you've discussed the plan with them on and off through the years. In most families, an adult child is the executor of the estate: explaining to all of your children how and why you have chosen your executor gives everyone a chance to express their feelings about it, and betters the chance of everyone working harmoniously later on. (See page 122 for resources on how to find professionals to help with these matters.)

▶ **Tell your kids what your wishes—and also your fears—are.** If you're worried about family disharmony in dividing up the estate you may be able to minimize the possibility by the nature of the written agreements you make in advance. But you can also talk to your kids about what your feelings are. Do you have an opinion as to who should be involved in dividing the contents of the house (or anyone who should not)? Do you have strong feelings against having your belongings sold off? Let your kids know what your wishes are. They may have helpful ideas about how to avoid ruffled feathers, or how to help smooth the part of the process you are concerned about.

▶ **Tell them where you've hidden special things!** Be sure to tell at least one person the location of any important documents, sentimental treasures, or anything else you might want them to be able to find should you die or be suddenly disabled. One family we know almost lost several pieces of jewelry that had both financial and sentimental value, when the very convincing book safe in which they were hidden almost went off to the library. If you have collections be sure someone knows where the inventory is kept. And if you have the habit of stuffing cash or other valuables into odd, out-of-the-way places, don't be embarrassed to tell your family. It's better for them to know now than for valuable things to be thrown out in ignorance later.

▶ **Take the time to share stories.** One of the most precious things children can inherit is a strong sense of family history. Taking the time to share stories is a wonderful gift you can give your children. If the chipped milk pitcher reminds you of long-ago breakfasts by the fire, tell your kids about it. The pitcher may not be worth much, but the story is priceless. And stories, unlike physical possessions, don't need to be divided—in fact, they can multiply and be enjoyed by everyone in the family for generations to come.

TALKING WITH YOUR PARENTS

It's at least as hard for your parents to talk about this as it is for you. Begin the conversation slowly, and be considerate of their feelings as you go.

▶ **Start now.** Whatever your parents' age, it's time for them to start talking about the eventual disposition of their belongings. Encourage them; let them know you're ready to have this conversation whenever they are.

▶ **Listen more than you talk.** Let your parents do most of the talking. Make the discussion a dialogue, not a lecture.

▶ **Ask how you can help.** Your parents may have their own ideas about how to get the process started, and how they would like you to help. They may or may not want your opinions; they may, or may not, want your physical help.

▶ **Be prepared with your suggestions.** If your parents are at a loss as to how to start, have some concrete suggestions for them. Even if they don't accept your ideas, hearing yours may help them to formulate their own.

▶ **Ask questions.** As you talk about specific items, ask about any special memories they may evoke. You may be surprised at the details of family history that will emerge.

Preparing for the Day

Regardless of how you come to the conclusion that it's time to empty the house and move on, once the decision has been made, there are several steps you can take to get started.

The first is to figure out where you are going, since what you will be able to take with you depends—a lot—on that decision. Moving from a large family home to a small apartment means one level of downsizing, and moving from a small apartment to a nursing home means another. If you know where you're going, you'll have a much easier time figuring out what is sensible to keep, and what you will need to get rid of. Having a floor plan of the place you're moving to, and important measurements, will help a lot in figuring out which large items you will be able to bring with you.

A friend drew a floor plan of our new apartment and it turned out to be such a helpful idea that I heartily recommend it to anyone moving from a house to an apartment. I measured my furniture and used the floor plan to see where it would fit. Since we don't have a dining room in the apartment, I didn't think I would be able to take our breakfront. Using the floor plan enabled me to see where it would fit. And I'm so glad because I would be lost without it.

The timetable is important as well. Professional organizers will tell you that it's best to have at least six months for such a move, but whatever your timetable is, you should get a calendar for this use only, and then plan your strategy. You might mark off "D-Day" (for decision made), and "M-Day" (for moving), then mark (in pencil) the day the necessary steps will be made, moving both backward and forward. Assign various members of the family to whatever tasks they can be responsible for, and decide tentative dates for any sales you might have, and deadlines for the other tasks you will need to accomplish. If you have no

experience estimating the time needed for big jobs, take a general tip from freelancers and independent contractors: figure out the time you realistically think you will need, and then multiply it by at least two!

If possible, the move to another location should be completed with plenty of time to spare before the belongings that remain behind in the house are divided among others and removed from the premises. As anyone who has ever moved knows, moving is an exhausting, confusing, and emotionally upsetting ordeal. For a person who is moving out of a beloved home they've lived in for many years, it is all the more so. Ideally, the people making the move should be given the time to settle into their new surroundings, and make sure that they have taken with them all they want, before the contents of their previous home are taken away. You don't want to regret having given away too much too soon, or to have important things lost in the shuffle.

AGREEING ON A FAMILY PLAN

Sometimes there's no time to prepare; a death or a severe health crisis came up suddenly and unexpectedly, and the family now has to dispose of the family home and everything in it on a tight schedule. If you are an only child, or the sole survivor in the family, you probably have a daunting task before you, and the best first step might very well be to look for help. For most people, this is too big a task to tackle alone. You might turn to close relatives or friends of the family; or you may want to find professional help.

If you are one of several children in the family, it's important for you and your siblings to take the time to talk about how to proceed. All interested parties should be in general agreement before launching into action. Even if some of those siblings are far away and not able to be involved in the nitty-gritty, have a discussion with *everyone* involved, so that any special requests can be considered, and hard feelings can be avoided down the line. Nobody should actually remove anything from the house (except any personal belongings that may have been stored there) until and unless consent has been given by all of the parties involved.

*B*e sure that you talk through the logistics and details about not just who gets what, but who does what. It's also important for everyone to respect the fact that not everyone feels the same, and give each other some slack.

NOTE: When a house has to be emptied for whatever reason, whatever is in the house belongs to that person, or to their estate, unless it has specifically been given to another person as a gift. Children or other heirs should not assume that everything in the house automatically belongs to them. The person vacating the house, or their estate, may have financial obligations that need to be settled first.

When my mother died, and my father was preparing to move out of the house, my siblings all started taking things for themselves and giving things away, right after the funeral. It was upsetting for me, not so much because I resented any of them having any of the things they took, but I did resent them rushing the process. I would have felt much better about it all if we had sat down together and talked it through, so that each of us had a chance to say what things we would like to keep from the home we grew up in together. I felt robbed, not so much of the few things I would have liked, but of the chance to move through this process together as a family.

DIVIDING UP THE BELONGINGS: A FEW RIGHT WAYS

There's no doubt about it. This is probably the one area most fraught with emotional difficulty, and the area into which even fairly harmonious and smoothly functioning families can easily fall into traps and find themselves fighting, even if they enter the process with all the best intentions.

Marlene Stum, a professor of family social science who has studied families going through this process, discovered six main pitfalls that many families fall into. "Not understanding how sensitive a process this can be for some people; failing to talk through goals, and make sure that everyone's goals are compatible; failing to agree on what 'fair' means; assuming that various things have the same meaning, or lack of meaning, for everyone; not being aware of all the various methods for dividing things that exist; and failing to manage conflict." Her work led to the creation of *Who Gets Grandma's Yellow Pie Plate?* a workbook she and her colleagues at the University of Minnesota developed that helps families come to terms with some of the issues in play, and offers suggestions for constructive ways to approach them. When asked what advice she would give families who are about to start emptying a home, Stum says, "Know that some conflict is normal, and to be expected. Take your time, and don't try to rush through the job."

Talking with Your Siblings (or others)

When you are emptying a house together with other family members, it is important to first define, and then work together toward common goals. You may need to agree to disagree about some things. But try to affirm everyone's right to help decide on the process and goals. Here are some suggestions to help cultivate a spirit of give and take.

▶ **Keep your eyes on the prize.** This is not a contest to see who can get the most stuff. Remember that the future harmony of family relationships is also at stake. Which is more important?

▶ **Avoid power struggles.** If the first foray into any particular discussion raises hackles, back off and try again later when everyone's had a chance to think about it and calm down.

▶ **Acknowledge the past, but look to the future.** Be aware of any unfinished business that may be left over from your childhood, and try to keep it from getting in the way of constructive communication now.

▶ **Respect each other's differences.** Understand the fact that not everyone will feel the same way you do about your family's shared history or possessions. There may be a variety of ways to approach distributing things, and everyone needs to be able to make suggestions about how to proceed.

▶ **Make choices.** Think about what one special item in your family's home best symbolizes the way you feel about your family. This will help you gain perspective about everything else.

▶ **Ask each other what is fair.** Everyone has a different idea of fairness, and the answers you get may surprise you—and might even make it easier to divide up the possessions.

▶ **Share your memories.** Talking about your common history and hearing the different ways each member of the family experienced the "same" thing can further understanding and help strengthen bonds. It may also make the task of dividing up the stuff easier and more fun, or at least a bit less tedious.

I really didn't know until I started emptying out my father's house just how emotionally charged, and how emotionally draining this process is. It took me by surprise. Several of my siblings couldn't deal with it at all. They just stayed away, and let me and my brother do it all. We kept inviting them to come, and finally I realized, "They just can't do it. They can't deal with it at all." So I picked out a few special things for each of them, and sent those to them. They appreciated that.

Someone we spoke to who has been through the process of emptying a house several times stressed the importance of good communication among involved parties from the very beginning. "Try to all get together face to face—a lot is lost in the written word, or the quick phone call," she said, adding, "Every member involved should be as open and honest as possible, and the 'by laws' of the operation should be carefully discussed, agreed upon, and then stuck to. Do not bring baggage from some other dealings within the family to the process—try to deal only with the move, and the division of the property."

It's very difficult. You have all these undividable objects, and trying to figure out what to do with them all seems to bring out a hidden wealth of competition, stored-up resentment, all kinds of traps to fall into with members of your family.

The two most basic questions that need to be dealt with are: Who gets what? and Who decides? There are a number of "right" ways to go about finding the answers to these questions. Clear communication from the original owner and advance planning are the best ways to make the answers clear. But when the answers have not been clearly provided, taking the time to discuss various options with other family members and making sure everyone involved is on board and in general agreement is all the more important.

When my brothers and I emptied our mother's home, we didn't invite our wives, or the grandchildren, to be involved in the process of dividing up the things. It seemed simpler that way, and it worked well for us.

The monetary value attached to items in the family estate may or may not be of critical importance. Experts who deal with these matters on a regular basis have plenty of stories about families torn apart by petty bickering over items of negligible value. After all, if money were the only thing that mattered, the whole thing would be much simpler. You could just sell everything, and equally divide the proceeds among the survivors. But the process of dismantling a family home is far from cut-and-dried; it is one that tends to awaken whatever unresolved emotional issues are most alive in your family. If your brother has always felt that "Mom always liked you best," or your sister resents the fact that you're always the one to take charge, now is the time those feelings are likely to come to the surface. Besides that, many of the objects you will be dealing with are loaded with emotional significance and packed with either precious or traumatic memories. The very fact that you are having to get rid of many of them means you have to face the fact that, for better or worse, it is the end of an era, so the process of sifting through them all is just not easy.

If there is valuable jewelry, antiques, collectibles, or artwork, you may want to have them appraised (see page 30), though knowing the monetary value of the items may not necessarily help you in deciding how to dispose of them. Different families handle this matter differently: one way is to divide up the most valuable items among the children so that each child receives objects worth approximately equal amounts; another is to sell the most valuable pieces, and divide the profits equally. Items that have both sentimental and monetary value present a special challenge. In some families, siblings would not mind seeing each other keep valuable family heirlooms to pass down in the family, but would feel quite resentful if the recipient then turned around and decided to sell

Creating a Visual Record

Insurance companies recommend that homeowners keep an inventory of household goods, with photos of the items. Such a list can be helpful when it comes to dispersing the items in a home as well. Make a page for each room in the house, with numbered columns, listing the item ("bureau"), a description ("4-drawer oak chest, 30 inches long"), its history or provenance ("wedding gift" or "purchased when Susie was born" or "belonged to Great-aunt Madeleine"), and any additional comments ("For my granddaughter Isabel"; or "Please have this appraised and sold, with the profits divided equally among my children"; or "Ask cousin Josh if he would like this—his mother gave it to us"). You may leave the spaces in the last column blank if you want your children and grandchildren to decide which pieces interest them the most.

Take photographs of the items, and number the photographs to correspond with the list. If you are using a digital camera, you can create an electronic record with photos and descriptions, and then send them to members of your family via e-mail.

The visual record can be used to help sort through and assign belongings to various members of the family in advance. Each child and/or grandchild in the family can be given a copy and asked to mark those items they would like to have. The record will also come in handy when siblings are actually dividing up the estate. Each person can record which items they are taking, helping to ensure the items are being divided up fairly. It may seem that one person is getting more than the others because she's been more vocal, but a look at the list will help assure each person involved that he or she is getting a fair share.

them. In other families, it might not matter. The important thing is to talk it over together as a family, and decide what your ground rules, and your family's way of handling the matter, will be.

We used colored stickers to indicate which of our kids wanted which items. We marked the things we wanted to keep with black stickers, and then gave each of them a different color. They marked anything they wanted with their colored stickers, and if an item had more than one sticker on it, they had to negotiate with each other to figure out who got what. We just stayed out of it, and they worked it out on their own.

Writing It Down

In dividing an estate, siblings often get into arguments over theoretical suppositions about what their parents "would have wanted." One way of avoiding such arguments in the future is for you to make your wishes known ahead of time. The will is important, and verbal communication is great. But family property is often disbursed before the will is read, and verbal promises are, as the old saw goes, worth about as much as the paper they're written on. (Disputing whose memory of verbal promises is better, or which verbal promise was the most recent, is also a common starting point for arguments within the family.)

In some families, the parents write a letter stating their bequests for special items like the family Bible, an antique dining-room table, a silver tea set, the father's army jacket, favorite books, or other things that have special meaning. Such a letter should be signed, dated, and witnessed. A copy of the letter can be attached to the will, but copies should also be sent to each of the recipients listed in the letter so that everyone knows the givers' wishes before the will is read.

Family lore says my aunt and uncle were a love match from the day they met. When my aunt passed away, my uncle had her diamond engagement ring made into a man's ring that he wore every day. He told me that he was leaving the ring to his nephew. When my uncle died, the executor of his will, his lawyer, had no record of the bequest. Sadly, the ring was sold along with his other possessions, and the money was divided among all the nieces and nephews.

If there are items that you suspect may be contested, or may cause family friction, and you have a strong preference about where they should end up, but prefer not to discuss the matter with your children, assigning the recipient in a will is a good way to make your wishes known. But you may want to take steps to make sure that the item does not "disappear" somehow before the will is read.

I had a large lined notebook in which I wrote down what each of our four children had taken for themselves, and when. I had a page for each of them, and in addition to the list of items they took, I also made notes about who else might have wanted the item. The actual division of our possessions at the time we emptied the house went pretty smoothly, but as the months passed, and one or another of our children had second thoughts or regrets, we were able to refer to the notebook and see how and why things had been dispersed as they were. This helped, as they went about making trades until everyone was happy.

If you prefer not to think about such things in detail, or do not have any strong preferences, you might make a general directive that will give your children guidance in making those decisions themselves when the time comes. One mother we know stipulated in her will that if any two of her children began to argue over the disposition of a particular item, whoever was involved in the argument would instantly be disqualified from ownership. "This really helped us keep things in perspective," one of the daughters remembers. "We knew that family harmony was much more important to our mother than material objects, and her message, coming from beyond the grave, helped us to keep what was most important always in mind, too."

Marking Possessions

Many families begin the process of assigning inherited items, both large and small, years before anyone is thinking about actually dismantling the home. This is one way of gently and realistically preparing everyone for the eventual day, while making it less painful and confusing when it comes. It's a kind of half-step that allows you to continue living in your home, surrounded by the possessions that give you pleasure, while you begin the process of passing them on to others.

There are various ways of going about this. Some people actually mark items on the back or on the bottom with masking tape, or attach notes to items tucked away in closets or cupboards. (You may change your mind later, so be wary of permanent marking methods like nail polish.) In some families, simply saying, "I'd like you to have the silverware someday," may be a good first step. If the intended recipient says, "You know, that's really nice, but I think I'd rather have Grandpa's violin," or "I know Kathy really wants the silverware, and that's fine with me," there's time to adjust your thoughts on the matter and consider your second choice. Even if you start the process with a conversation, it's best to eventually put your thoughts in writing one way or another— whether it's in the will, on a piece of masking tape, or marked on the

back of the item with marker pen. (Every family can devise its own method, taking into account unique family dynamics and habits.) This makes your intentions perfectly clear, and the clearer things are when the day comes to divide the estate, the less likely disagreements will erupt when everyone's feeling tired, bereft, and out of sorts. Try not to fall into the trap of gender stereotyping as you think about dispersing special things, automatically giving jewelry and china to daughters, tools and golf clubs to sons. Your son may like to be able to pass on special jewelry to his daughter one day; your daughter may need a nice set of tools if she's just moved into her first house.

As we were emptying out one closet, we found a plain brown box containing six glasses with Christmas scenes on them tucked into the back of the shelf. On the box was a handwritten message from my mother. "These glasses belong to Debra," it said. She had written our names on various items, or on pieces of tape attached to the objects, or had tucked little notes into boxes. Finding these notes made the sorting process so much easier, and more meaningful, too. We knew that family items were going to the person my mother had decided should have them.

Trash or Treasure?

For many people, hiring an appraiser to place a value on family possessions may seem a bit intimidating at first. Is it really worth the time and money? Is our furniture really antique? Is the Red Wing pottery valuable to collectors? A professional appraiser can answer all of these questions, and more.

An appraiser can give you the value of a single piece, or can go through the entire house (a "look-see") to tell you which pieces may be valuable. The value of an item is determined by its condition, its rarity, and its provenance or history. Stories passed down in the family about the original source of items, however, are not always accurate, says Helaine Fendelman, host of the popular PBS show, *Treasures in Your Attic,* coauthor of *Price It Yourself!* and past president of the Appraisers Association of America. So you will need more than family lore to establish provenance.

An appraiser will supply you with what is known in the antiques business as "comparative market value," that is, the approximate value of an object based on recent prices realized for similar items. This is different than the auction value, the value that an expert estimates an item *might* bring at auction. (A third valuation, the fair market value (FMV), used by the IRS and for charitable contributions, is the price the item would sell for in the open market; it is usually 40 percent of the insurance value, which is the replacement cost of an item.)

A good appraiser, according to Fendelman, is someone who is sensitive and caring and who understands the financial responsibility of giving an accurate appraisal. Appraisers will charge a flat fee or by the hour. (It is illegal to charge a percentage of the item being evaluated, since this could lead to an artificial increase in its appraised value.) The person hiring the appraiser needs to trust him or her, and accept their expertise, so it's important to hire someone you feel comfortable with, someone you trust around your family's items, and someone you feel is honest. (Beware of an appraiser who asks to buy the piece.)

While some appraisers simply assign a dollar value to objects, most will also shepherd you through the selling process by suggesting the best place to sell—to an antiques store, dealer, consignment shop, or through an auction—and then helping you negotiate with the seller (if that is what you want). The appraiser will also know if the object is a collectible, and can advise you on which items are worth holding onto for a while—which things are likely to go up in value, and which are not.

Sometimes an appraiser will suggest that the item has little or no monetary value and that it would be more appropriate to donate it to charity than to try to sell it. If this happens, don't be discouraged. As Fendelman says, "Every object in the world has a value; you just may not like the value it has." And of course, the process of appraising has nothing to do with the emotional or sentimental value of an item.

To find a professional appraiser, ask your lawyer, banker, real estate agent, or friends for a referral. The appraiser should ask probing questions in the initial interview (Where did you get the piece? How much did you pay for it? Do you have a receipt? Are you aware if this has been restored?). You can ask the appraiser probing questions, too. Ask what qualifies him or her to appraise your items. No one is an expert in all areas; if what you want valued is furniture, you want an appraiser with experience in that area. You can also inquire if the appraiser is a member of a professional organization, and what qualifications the organization requires of its members.

Can you estimate what something is worth without a professional appraiser? Certainly you can do research in the library, on the Internet, or in museums, and you can browse through antique shops and attend auctions to get an idea of what your items are worth. (See page 118 for books on the subject.) Researching the history and value of a family item can be an enjoyable pastime and the knowledge you gain can help you decide if you want to hire a professional appraiser.

There are on-line appraisals, but how good they are depends on the quality of the photographs and the expertise of the appraiser. For best results, take photos in good light, from different angles, and include close-ups of details. On-line appraisals can give a good idea of an object's value. If you later decide to sell the item, you may then hire an appraiser who can see the object in person.

No Time Like the Present

Another way to go about dividing the estate is to go ahead and give things to the ones you'd like to see have them now rather than later. There are several advantages to this, and the longer you live, the more it makes sense to take this step. If you want your daughter to have the silverware, why not give it to her now? If she's the one hosting the annual family Thanksgiving dinner, doesn't it make sense for her to have it? When is the last time you actually used it? Do you see yourself using it again? Asking yourself these kinds of questions may lead you to realize that in some ways the torch has already passed on to the next generation, and that the best way of enjoying family traditions and special things is to pass them along now, while you're alive and can still enjoy them together. If resentments over your decisions surface, you also still have time to explain your intentions to the other children, and make amends or changes. (There may be tax implications if the items you are giving away are very valuable. Ask your attorney or accountant for advice.)

My mom divvied up her most valuable things before she died. And she didn't just hand them over to us—she gave them as Christmas, birthday, and anniversary presents. She actually joked that not having to shop for presents was so wonderful, she wished she had started doing it sooner. So the advice would be, find creative and joyous ways to give away your possessions, and save your loved ones potential headaches.

READY, SET . . . GO!

The truth is that, even with plenty of advance planning and all the time in the world, the final steps in this process are inevitably both physically and emotionally demanding. There's no way to guarantee that you and your family will be able to get through this job with no hard feelings generated, and no emotional outbursts. In fact, there are almost certain to be such moments as you go about the task. But there are better and worse ways of getting through those moments when they occur; and much of this book will focus on identifying what the better ways are. We talked to a lot of people who came up with creative and effective solutions for working out whatever problems they encountered, by applying plenty of patience and understanding, as well as a sense of humor. It is our hope that, by hearing their stories and suggestions, you and your family will be able to minimize the heartache and stress, and that you might even have a little bit of fun along the way.

So, once you've had time to develop an overall plan, talk things over with each other, and set some ground rules, it's time to roll up your sleeves and begin the task.

Smart Questions to Ask

- ☑ Has everyone in the family been consulted, and informed, that we are about to start emptying the house?
- ☑ Have we made a family plan for how to go about this process? Has everyone agreed to it?
- ☑ Have we set a date when the process will begin? Is it clear to everyone who will be involved?
- ☑ Have we talked about how to handle any disagreements or disputes that may arise in the process?
- ☑ Have we dealt with any disagreements about any of the above as well as we can? If we are not all in agreement, do we at least have a consensus that the process should begin?

CHAPTER 2

Sorting It Out

WHEN WE STARTED WORKING on this book, someone who had just emptied two houses herself said to us, a bit impatiently, "All you have to do is just plunge in." The problem is, when faced with a task as enormous and as emotionally loaded as emptying the family home, some people plunge head-first into the deep end of the pool, while others sit on the edge and gingerly dip their toes in. The way you go about getting started is as personal as the decisions you make about what you keep. To complicate matters, different members within a family almost always have different styles of dealing with the same situation. The challenge is to get everyone to work together in a spirit of cooperation, both efficiently and harmoniously, while leaving room for everyone to deal with his or her own idiosyncrasies.

Not So Fast!

Throwing things away (other than obvious trash such as spoiled food in the refrigerator, out-of-date medicines, and burned-out lightbulbs) should not be your first step. The first step is to sort, and as you're sorting, consult with each other about what to do with it all.

If you plan on holding an estate sale or auction at your house, ask a couple of professionals to come in and evaluate the estate before you start throwing things out or hauling them away. Part of their professional expertise is knowing what kinds of "worthless" items can actually be worth a little, or a lot. It is surprising, to say the least, to learn what kinds of things can actually be big sellers at estate sales. For example:

- (Certain) old cereal boxes
- Old (even used and worn) rag rugs
- Old linens
- Empty perfume bottles
- Vintage clothing (including clothing from the 70s and 80s)
- Postcards (even ones that are written on)

Also we have been told by many people that money, important papers, and other treasures are often found hidden within stacks of papers, inside seemingly "empty" envelopes, in the pages of books, in the pockets of clothing, and in other unlikely spots.

Finally, many things tossed willy-nilly into the Dumpster—from old Christmas cards and maps to sewing-machine manuals and sales receipts—could be of interest to your local historical society. (See more about this on page 94.)

Getting Started

Having said that, it is true that at some point you do just have to "plunge in." One way to get started is to divide everything into three categories:

- what you (or someone else in your family) definitely want to save
- what you are unsure about
- what nobody wants, and which must go

As you are sorting, these categories can be divided into several smaller, more manageable subcategories. What you definitely want to save may be divided into groups: a pile of items for each of the siblings to take home; things you want to give to relatives; things you would like to return to the original owner (like the painting your mother's best friend gave to her); items you want to have appraised; and things that may have historical significance. The items that nobody wants will be divided as well, into things that will be sold (to an antiques store or consignment shop, at a yard sale, auction, or on-line); things that will be donated; and things that will go straight to the trash.

We went through my mother's house room by room, and pulled every single thing out of each drawer, closet, from under the bed—everything. Then we laid it all out so we could see what was there. Next we went through everything, and everybody took what they wanted. (This was not big or valuable items like furniture or paintings, just the "stuff" stuff.) Then, with whatever was left over, we asked, Do we give it to friends? Save it for Christmas? Give it to the Goodwill? We decided then and there, and we stuck to it. We put the rest in boxes and took it all away, according to the decisions we had made.

Whether you are sorting through the house slowly, one closet at a time, or emptying the entire house in a week, you will want to take the time to reconsider your decisions as you go along. Given time to think about it most people find that many items change category. It's possible you will decide to keep some things you originally thought you'd throw away, but more likely you will find that you can part with more than you thought you could when you first started.

When my two sisters and I were breaking up my mother's house of 40-plus years, we of course came upon things that more than one of us thought we couldn't live without. After the first few snide comments, we made a "fight shelf" for the disputed items. The "fight shelf" grew into the "fight room," and by the end of the summer there was quite a stash of memorabilia, none of which had much intrinsic value, but all of which held emotional and political power.

On an early fall morning we went to divvy up the goods, when we were all fresh and cool. We drew straws to determine the order of picks. After each of us had appropriated our first few choices in an orderly fashion, the pickings began to look a little slim. I picked up a very ugly tray and tried to recall who had fought over such a piece of trash. We couldn't remember! One by one we inspected the remaining items, getting more and more amused by what we had once thought was worth fighting over. We ended up laughing uncontrollably. The rest of the contents of the room went to Goodwill, where I hope they found new owners with as much possessive enthusiasm as we had once had.

Retirees who are moving from a house to an apartment will want to first decide what to bring with them. In addition to whatever furniture and household items you will need in the new place, you will want to keep at least some of the things that give you comfort and that will make the apartment feel like home. Setting aside these items is a good first step. And don't forget to take into account your pet's needs when planning the move. If you are bringing your dog or cat with you to the new place, don't throw out their old beds yet: pets also need to make the transition gradually.

If you are not pressed for time, you can afford to start small. Clean out a kitchen drawer, go through the linen closet, or empty one box in the attic. As you are going through the house, gather together similar items so you can see what you have. If you have a great quantity of one type of item—decorative throw pillows, vases, or tools—get them all together in one place, choose your favorites, and set aside the rest.

When we were moving from our family home to an apartment we asked our two grown daughters to sort through their personal things. The older one said we could just throw everything out—that if anything was worth saving, she had already taken it. Fortunately, she was around when our younger daughter started going through the files of school papers and childhood keepsakes. They laughed and reminisced and had a wonderful time. Our older daughter ended up keeping more than she thought she would, and more than our younger daughter.

This is a good time to set aside personal items—photographs, jewelry, important books, and papers such as report cards, diplomas, and letters—in a category of their own. Make separate piles that each of the adult children in the family can transfer to their homes. Also set aside family memorabilia, such as immigration papers, marriage certificates, medals or other awards, and anything else that has a name on it.

You can start by sorting out items that are definitely going to be given away or sold—kitchen utensils, old towels, old books, tools, kids' toys and games, clothing, area rugs, picture frames—although many families may find it difficult to agree on which objects are the *definite* give-aways. It's important to allow everyone involved individual veto power over what can be tossed, and to respect each other's feelings, though you may want to attach an "okay-then-take-it-to-your-house" clause in order to keep your primary goal from being undermined. In any case, the more the easier stuff is weeded out in the beginning, the fewer items there will be to have to decide on later.

There are many ways to begin the process and it really doesn't matter where you start. Just start!

My brother and I have had a lot of trouble respecting each other's territory as we go through the mountains of things in my mother's house. Whenever he gets bogged down going through the old tools in the basement, he comes to where I am, agonizing over old clothing worn by our mother and grandmother, and says, "Why don't you just toss all this stuff?" I really resent that, so then I go to the basement and start picking up old tools and saying "Why do we need this?" Then *he* gets upset.

CONSIDERING STORAGE

Storing an item, or many items for that matter, is a personal decision and whether it's the right thing to do for you depends on a number of factors.

We've heard many discouraging stories on the subject—about items temporarily stored in a friend's garage that stayed there for years; of boxes put in someone's basement that just disappeared; of

To Store or Not to Store

Deciding whether or not to store items can be difficult. On the one hand, you don't want to simply defer decisions by postponing the moment of truth. On the other hand, temporarily storing some items can be a good interim step for many families. Here is a list of questions to ask yourselves to help you determine whether using storage is the right step for you.

■ Does the item have practical value? Sentimental value? No value? Are you waiting for it to go up in value?

■ What is the cost—personal as well as financial—of renting a storage space? Of using a friend or relative's garage or basement? Will the cost of monthly storage put a dent in your budget? Will using a friend's basement begin to wear on your friendship?

■ Who is in charge of the storage space? Will all interested parties have access to it? Is everything well labeled?

■ Are the conditions in the storage place appropriate for the items you want to store? Will wood warp? Will paper deteriorate? Will fabric rot?

■ Do you have a plan for the items? Are you storing them until you can have a yard sale, sell them at auction, sort through them with your family? Is the plan open-ended, or do you have a specific time in mind?

■ Be honest. Are you storing items simply because you cannot make a decision about them? If so, how will having more time help you?

paying monthly storage fees for years while deciding what to do with certain things, and then ending up by throwing most of them away. We've also heard positive stories about people who chose to store items until they could be shipped to a family member or sold at auction, or of storing family furniture just a few months, until all the siblings could have a look at it. If you have to empty an entire house quickly, you may decide to store some things until you have the time to sort through them all.

If you do decide to store some things for a while, in addition to the traditional self-storage units to which you haul the goods and lock them away yourself, some companies now offer "door-to-store" service, in which they bring mobile storage units to the house, leave them for you to fill, and pick them up and take them to the storage unit when you're ready. For families overwhelmed with the task of emptying a house on a tight schedule, that extra measure of service can be very helpful.

MAKING IT WORK

It's a big job to sort through an entire house, especially if it is necessary to go through everything in a fairly short time. But there are ways to make the job easier.

Plan at least several sessions. It took years to gather all the possessions in the house; it's only natural that it will take quite a while to sort through them all. Don't put extra pressure on yourself, or criticize siblings who are dealing with it, thinking it can all be done overnight. Decisions made in haste are often regretted. If the house has to be emptied instantly, you may have to buy time by storing some things or dispersing others among yourselves. It's best not to postpone the decisions, but you have to give yourself time to do it right.

Choose a date, and notify everyone in the family of what you're doing. This may seem obvious, but make sure that all the people who need to know that the sorting process is beginning are consulted and informed before it starts. Agree on a date that is convenient for everyone who wants to be there. This may include both parents, all sib-

lings, and perhaps spouses or other close relatives. Don't allow one person to start going through items alone unless you have all agreed that this is how the process will begin.

Be prepared to work. Wear comfortable clothing, and have all the supplies you'll need on hand. You will need garbage bags, boxes, string, scissors, markers, plastic bags, tape, and perhaps colored stickers or some other means for marking items. Bring along file folders and labels if you have a lot of papers to sort through. You might also want to have archival storage containers ready to load with old photographs, letters, and heirloom-quality clothing or other textiles. (See page 124.) And you will want to have packing materials available, especially for fragile items. These materials can often be purchased from truck and trailer rental companies for less than they would cost in an office-supply store. Or you may be able to order materials and have them delivered to you for even less. Check the yellow pages, or on-line under Moving Supplies.

$\mathcal{J}$ carried a canvas bag around with me all the time, wherever I went. In the bag I had all my essentials: a camera, film, a couple of extra pens and pencils, a notebook (slips of paper get lost), an envelope to put stray pieces of paper and notes in, Scotch tape, paper-clips, rubber bands, colored stickers, measuring tape, and a magnifying glass (to read manufacturing marks on silverware, pottery, etc.). I also put any broken or odd pieces of things I came across into this bag, and then when I passed by a special box I had set aside for broken and odd pieces, would toss them into it. By the end of the process, many of the broken bits had been reunited with their original pieces.

Be organized. Work in one room at a time. If several siblings are working together, you can "divide and conquer"; one can work in the kitchen, another in the bedroom. It's best if you can keep from switching areas. You will squander your energy by trying to approach too many areas at once, and may very likely be simply trying to avoid making decisions that you eventually will have to make.

Break large tasks into smaller, more manageable parts.
Cleaning out the basement, for example, is too large a task. Start by examining what's there, and creating categories. Put tools in one place, sports equipment in another, entertainment items in yet another. Then sort through each category. If going through the clothing is too overwhelming, divide it into groups: coats, day wear, casual and sportswear, seasonal, shoes, accessories. Keep sorting until you have categories of a manageable size.

Check everywhere. Pull out drawers, pull up drawer lining, leaf through books, go through all boxes and bags even if it looks as though they contain nothing but junk. People often hide things in out-of-the-way places and then forget about them—so inspect everything.

My husband taught me to be careful going through things. After emptying my mother's house of furniture and clothing, we were going through the stuff in the basement. I saw my husband going through a basket full of plastic bags that my mother had saved. I said "What are you doing? It's garbage. Just throw them out." Well, he continued to look and, at the bottom, found a bag with $1600 in twenty-dollar bills.

Keep things in order. If possible, set aside certain rooms as designated repositories for particular categories of sorted items. For example, you could put "items to keep" in a bedroom, "not-sure items" in the living room, and "items to go" in the den. For furniture that is too unwieldy to move, colored tags on each piece can clearly designate the category.

Check each other's work. Remember to let everyone "sign-off" before anything leaves the house or goes into the trash.

I knew we weren't all using the same operational definition of "junk" when I found, right in the top of a garbage bag on its way out of the house, the gold pin my mother had been given on her graduation from nursing school, engraved with her initials and the date, along with other trinkets she had kept in a box in her dresser drawer. We got together and agreed we had to slow things down and check each other's work, so that in our fervor to get rid of things we didn't need or want anymore, we didn't throw out things that were meaningful to some of us.

Accept help if it is offered, but don't be afraid to control the type of help you receive and the times you are open to it. Extended family can be very helpful in emptying out a family home, but there are some parts of the process in which the presence of others can be more unnerving than helpful. You don't want someone gleefully throwing away things you want to look through, or second-guessing decisions that are hard enough to make in the first place. If someone offers to help before you're ready for their help, tell them you appreciate the offer and you'll let them know when you're ready to call them in on the job. Then think ahead so that you will have tasks ready for them when they arrive.

Take time to mourn. We have rituals for mourning the death of a loved one, but we do not have any prescribed way to mourn the break-up of a family home. Everything in our homes has a story attached to it. In order to give things away, some people need to find a way to separate the memories from the objects. While you are sorting through things, as much as possible, take the time to remember the good times, and talk about them with each other. Remember that you can keep the memories even as you let go of the items.

Enjoy yourself. Bring along some homemade cookies to snack on. Play some of those old records as you sort through them, and sing along as you work. Does the old 8mm projector work? Why not find out by screening one of those old reels, and get a laugh (or a cry) while you're at it? Allow time for lunch and coffee breaks during the day—these are ideal times for assessing where you are, consulting with each other about next steps, and sharing the memories jogged during your labors.

At the end of the day, order some take-out food, take pride in what you have accomplished, and try not to worry about what remains to be done. Remember that emptying even one overstuffed kitchen drawer is an accomplishment and gets you closer to your goal.

Smart Questions to Ask

☑ Does the cost of shipping and/or storing an item (or items) make sense from an economic point of view? (Could I buy new items of the same or better quality for less than the cost of packing and shipping the old ones?)

☑ If I throw this out in a fit of exhaustion or annoyance, will my children or grandchildren regret it? Will my brother (or my uncle) resent my doing so?

☑ Am I throwing this out because I really don't want it, or because I don't know what to do with it?

☑ Will I use this item? Do I have an emotional attachment to it? Or am I holding on to it simply because it belonged to my parents?

☑ Am I the caretaker for all of our family's stuff? Can someone else in the family share this role?

☑ Can a decision about a disputed item, or issue within the family, wait? Why does it have to be decided right now? Can it wait an hour? A day? A week?

Is There a Clutterer in Your Closet?

You've heard the stories, about a house packed so full of stuff—most of it pure, unadulterated junk by anyone's standards—that you literally cannot walk through the rooms or find a chair that is free to sit on. And while most people's homes never get quite *that* bad, we all know someone who is a "pack rat," and for many of us that person is someone in our family.

Why is it so hard for some people to throw things away? Are they just lazy? Inherently disorganized? Willfully messy, and stubborn to boot?

The answer to these questions is probably not. For some people, hoarding or cluttering is actually a bona fide psychological disorder. Hoarding to this degree affects about 10 percent of Americans; the condition cuts across economic and class lines, and is found equally among males and females. It is more common in the current elderly population that came of age during the Depression and World War II years, and is definitely hereditary: 80 percent of all hoarders have a family history of cluttering.

As with most psychological conditions, there is a broad spectrum of symptoms, from a mere difficulty in getting rid of sentimental items to a pathological inability to throw away junk mail, old newspapers, packing materials, or egg crates, even if holding onto them means shunning social contact, compromising close family ties, or risking eviction from one's home. Often the behavior is almost completely irrational, but sometimes there is a twisted and irrefutable logic in why certain things have been kept, and often a painful emotional element. "You're throwing away my life!" one elderly mother we know protested when her daughter tried to make space by hauling out bags full of plastic bags.

When someone does have an extraordinarily difficult time parting with objects, what can family and friends do to help? Norma Thomas, a professor of social work at Widener University, who has studied the phenomenon of cluttering among the elderly, says that in many cases the best thing to do is to monitor the situation for any health and safety hazards, and try to ignore the mess. "If it's just a question of messiness, and the person who lives in that mess is content with it, you have to respect their right to live the way they want to. It's hard for people who don't have the problem themselves to understand that these seemingly worthless things represent something important to the person who can't let go of them. It could be a sense of security, it could be precious memories, it could be a lot of things." She recommends providing firm, but nonjudgmental assistance in dealing with any safety issues, and turning a blind eye to the rest.

If the person agrees to it, you can also help by going through piles of things with them, and tossing or taking things out of the house, with their consent. But asking them why they don't "just get rid of all this junk" is not helpful, and doing it for them without their consent can actually be detrimental to their mental health, not to mention your relationship with them. Without accompanying therapy of some kind, it is also highly ineffective—in most cases, a thorough housecleaning and "dejunking" session almost inevitably is followed by a resumption of the cluttering behavior within a very short period of time.

Clutterers need understanding, sensitive assistance with what is an extremely difficult task for them (i.e., getting rid of, or throwing out anything), and in some cases may benefit from professional help, or participation in a support group such as Clutterers Anonymous. (See page 122.)

If you find yourself in the unenviable position of pawing your way through a closet, a room, or a whole house that has been stuffed to the gills, take comfort in knowing that you're not alone. Don't despair, and do be careful—hidden within the piles of complete and total junk you may find unexpected treasures.

CHAPTER 3

Saving Precious Memories

AS YOU GO THROUGH THE house setting aside those things you want to keep, you will very likely come across items that need to be rescued or safeguarded from decay. Sometimes you will find items in such a state that you may think the best or only thing to do is to toss them, and you may be right. (But you could also be wrong, so don't be too hasty in your decision to toss anything that may have sentimental or potential historical value.) This chapter will provide some tips on how to arrest further deterioration of items that hold important family memories, while you figure out what to do with them next.

Don't forget that emptying the house can also be an opportune time to capture memories that are hiding in the hearts and minds of those who are still around, and to record and save those memories so that you can share them with generations to come.

PRESERVING FAMILY HEIRLOOMS

Heat, light, moisture, dust, dirt, insects and other pests, and excessive or careless handling are the main enemies of your family's sentimental treasures, whether they are photographs, home movies, important documents, christening cups and gowns, quilts, or antique toys. In general, the best environment for storage is one with a relatively constant, moderate temperature (65–75 degrees Fahrenheit is ideal) and humidity. This means that anything truly important to you should be kept either in special storage under climate-controlled conditions, or in the main living area of your home, rather than in an attic, garage, or basement where it is subject to fluctuations in temperature and humidity levels. Another enemy of long-term preservation is cramming too many mementos—whether they are textiles, photographs, or papers—into too small a space. Most materials are better off stored flat and loose, with room to breathe.

If you find precious family things that are damaged, it is almost always better to consult a professional conservator than to try to repair the damage yourself. The American Institute for the Conservation of Historic and Artistic Works (AIC) can help you find reputable professional conservators in your area. (See page 122.) The following is some *general* advice about how to properly handle and store items under relatively good conditions, so if there has been any damage or deterioration, it will not be compounded—and if there has not been, it will not begin now.

Photos and Written Documents

If you're dealing with a full house, chances are you will come across a lot of photographs, letters, and other paper documents as you open closet doors and sort through boxes. If you are lucky, these documents and photographs will have been properly stored and cared for all along, and all you will have to do is figure out where they go next. But most people are not that lucky. You are much more likely to find these things stored haphazardly, in inappropriate places or ways, and often in a deteriorating state. What do you do then?

The conservation and preservation of paper documents and photographs are specialized fields of expertise, and you can hardly be expected to know in a short time what some people devote their entire professional careers to. However, there are a few basic steps you can take to minimize damage and keep your precious family images and records in the best condition possible while you figure out what to do next.

If they are not already in archival-quality, acid-free storage containers—boxes, folders, or envelopes—transfer them to such containers. If you find photos and letters stored in old shoeboxes and don't have the money to spend on acid-free storage materials, you'll take one step toward preserving them by throwing out the old boxes (which will have begun the process of deterioration), and replacing them with new ones, according to Linda Edquist, conservator at the Smithsonian Institution's National Postal Museum. You can further protect precious memories by lining those boxes with unbleached muslin, archival paper, or Tyvek, which puts a protective barrier between the material you're trying to preserve and the acidic cardboard it's being stored in. (Old sheets or pillowcases, if they are clean and dry, will work just as well.) Old letters and notebooks could also be placed in a clean envelope made of an inert substance like Tyvek, and then placed in a box.

Store photographs and papers in a relatively cool, dry, and stable environment. Attics, basements, and garages, all places where old papers and photographs are frequently stored, are particularly bad choices, because they tend to be damp, exposed to extreme temperatures, and vulnerable to flooding. You want to find a place with relatively little air circulation. Place the photographs or letters in a tightly closed box that will protect the contents from dust and dirt, and keep the box in a closet, inside a trunk, or even under a bed.

Keep materials separated by type, as much as possible. This means storing newspaper articles, postcards, photographs, negatives, and letters in separate envelopes, folders, or boxes. Storing different media together—newsprint and photographs, for example—can cause unpredictable and harmful chemical reactions. In addition, different materials require different types of treatment and storage. (Buffered tissue paper is the best way of preventing acidification of newsprint and other kinds of paper; for photographs, unbuffered paper is better.) Old scrapbooks, which frequently include a mixture of newspaper articles, photographs, dried flowers, and other materials, present a particularly complicated conservation dilemma. For now, placing any old scrapbooks you find in large Tyvek envelopes, and storing them flat, is a good way to put them "on hold."

Glue, tape, paper clips, rubber bands, or any kind of adhesive material (including Post-it notes) should never be in direct contact with your photographs or documents. If you find photographs or documents fastened or labeled with these materials, gently remove the materials before placing the photos or documents in archival storage containers. But be careful—if it looks like the act of removing staples or paper clips will further damage the surface, leave that step for later.

Perhaps most important of all, whatever you do, be careful! When asked what one piece of advice or warning she would give to people who encounter precious family documents while emptying out a home, Edquist cautions, "You can do more damage to documents through mishandling them than they would suffer in another ten years if they were left alone sitting in the attic." So approach them with patience, and handle them with care. Be sure to work in an area that is

When is it Too Late?

What do you do when you find a box of old pictures, books, or baby clothing that is covered, or spotted, with mold? Do you have to toss everything out? Not necessarily, but you should isolate any items that contain active mold right away. If the mold damage is slight, and not active, you can place the items in sunlight for a short time until the mold spores are dry and can be easily brushed off the surface, using a clean, soft artists' brush. Linda Edquist, of the Smithsonian Institution's National Postal Museum, recommends placing objects with active mold into a zip-top bag and consulting an expert for advice on how to deal with them. (In addition to the delicate issue of preservation, there are health issues to consider: it is not healthy to breathe in mold spores.) You can find reputable conservators in your area by contacting the AIC, or asking for a reference at your local historical society. (See page 122.)

clean, and handle things only with clean hands. If you are handling photographs without gloves, it is extremely important to handle them by the edges only because oils from your fingers can cause permanent damage to the surface. If you do choose to wear gloves, use the powder-free latex type. Setting up a clean, dust-free area to work in is more important. If there are boxes full of old documents in the basement or

Memory's Friends and Enemies

If you know the best way and the best place to keep an item from your family's history, you can help extend its life so that the next generation can continue to enjoy it.

ENEMIES

- Heat, light, moisture, dust, dirt, insects and other pests
- Vinyl (PVC), self-adhesive items (Post-it notes, tape, magnetic photo albums), rubber bands, paper clips, glue
- Low-quality (highly acidic) paper, wood, mothballs
- Dirty hands, rough handling

FRIENDS

- Acid-free papers, unbleached muslin, Tyvek, inert plastics such as cellulose triacetate, Mylar polyester, polyethylene, and polypropylene
- Filtered glass (which screens out UV light)
- Flat, loose storage, moderate and relatively constant temperature and humidity
- Clean hands, cotton gloves
- Cautious, respectful handling

attic, you might want to set up a temporary worktable there, away from the activity in the main part of the house. Making photocopies or digital copies of old journals or letters that are beginning to fade is a good idea, but if you do so, be sure to make the copies onto high-quality, archival paper, and be very careful when handling the originals. (The brittle paper of old letters can easily break or crumble into pieces if it is not humidified before being unfolded and copied; carelessly opening notebooks, or pressing down too hard as you copy or scan them, can break the spine.)

Audio and Videotapes, Movies, and Slides

What do you do with the boxes of old slides, home movies, reel-to-reel audiotape, and other forms of now-obsolete recording media that you find in the basement or attic? If you have a playback device in the house that still functions, you can test the recordings on the spot, and at least know whether or not the images and sounds are still there. But, even if you find that the recording is in a good state of preservation, what should you do to save those images for the next generation? If you don't have a playback device, how can you find out if there are any retrievable images or sounds? If there are, how can you keep them safe from now on? And if you find tapes or slides that have been damaged, is there any way to restore them?

Videotape has been one of the most popular ways of recording precious family memories over the past twenty years, but, unfortunately, it is also a fragile and highly unstable storage medium. If you find videotapes that are ten years old or older, you should play them back (in a clean VCR) to see if they are still viable. If they are, they should be set aside and taken to experts where they can be copied onto new videotape, or transferred to another medium. (If the camera that was used to make the tapes in the first place is still in the house, don't get rid of it yet: you may be able to use it to create new copies of the tapes.) Old home movies present a bigger problem, since the projectors used to screen them are now more or less obsolete. If you do find old movies, the best thing to do is to get them to a professional who can convert them to videotape or another format.

NOTE: Most home movies and commercial movie reels made after the 1950s were made on safety film stock, and do not represent a fire hazard. However, old motion picture film made from nitrate is highly flammable. If you come across old commercial (35mm) film in a deteriorating state, and you think it may be made of nitrate, you should contact the local fire department immediately for advice about how to dispose of it safely.

Slides are a fairly stable photographic medium, though there will be some color distortion over time. If you find slides in good condition, make sure that they are stored properly, in protective pages made of a chemically stable polyester such as Mylar, and stored upright in a dust-free case or in archival-quality slide storage boxes.

Textiles and Clothing

Textiles and clothing present even more of a preservation dilemma than photographs and documents, since they are one-of-a-kind and are not reproducible. This means that you have to weigh the desire to maintain them over a long period of time against the desire to use them or have them out in the open, where they can be enjoyed.

Having said that, there are a number of fairly simple things you can do to lengthen the life of garments, samplers, quilts, and other special textiles. As with paper and photographs, the main enemies are heat, light, moisture, insects or other pests, and overcrowded storing conditions. And as with documents and photographs, improper storage and mishandling can cause unnecessary damage. Here are a few basic rules of care to follow:

Never wrap textiles in plastic. Over time, the synthetic materials used to make the plastic will melt and bleed into the textiles. In addition, because the plastic traps air, it can create condensation, which will further damage the fabric. Even wood can damage textiles over time, since it is acidic; so, while flat storage is good, wooden drawers should be lined with unbleached muslin or nonacidic paper to protect textiles from direct contact with the wood. Unbuffered tissue paper, which can be purchased from archival-storage suppliers, is safe for all fabrics. (Silk and wool should never be wrapped in buffered paper, but it is okay for cotton and linens.)

Check stored garments about once a year. Both folding textiles and hanging them will exert stress on the fibers. Garments that are folded and stored should be periodically checked to make sure there is no insect infestation, and then refolded. (It's best to try to fold garments along the seams.) Garments that are hung should be stored on polyester-padded wooden hangers with unbleached muslin covers.

Protect your textiles from bright light, whether from the sun or from an artificial source. A guest bedroom where there is no direct sunlight on the bed is an ideal way to both display and store a special

quilt. Hanging a quilt on a wall is another display option if it is in good condition, but hanging does pull and tug at the fibers. Creating a special sleeve through which a dowel or curtain rod can be fitted, or a special panel with Velcro attachments from which to hang the quilt, will minimize stress on the fibers.

If you find textiles that have been damaged by insects, mildew, or have spots or other damage, you may want to consult with a professional conservator about how to repair it. In general, the less handling the better: harsh soaps, dry cleaning, and rough handling can all cause further damage to textiles.

Jewelry, Silver, and Other Metal Objects

In some families, jewelry, antique toy cars, or swords owned by ancestors are valued family treasures. In others, the treasures may be grandmother's silverware, babies' christening cups, or guns. What all these objects have in common is the fact that they are made of metal.

Corrosion is the main enemy of metal objects: most metals will corrode on contact with water or even moisture in the air. Oily or sweaty hands can also damage metals: in fact, the distinct pattern of a person's fingerprint can corrode right into a metal surface. Metal objects should be handled with clean, white, cotton gloves. If gloves are not available, a clean, soft cloth placed between your hand and the metal will work just as well to protect it.

FINDING ARCHIVAL MATERIALS

As more people become interested in preserving their family history, an industry has grown up in response to the demand for archival-quality storage materials and containers. This is a good thing. However, buyer awareness and just a little bit of technical knowledge may be helpful in sorting out the real thing from sometimes dubious marketing claims and misleading product labeling.

First of all, you should know that "archival glue" and "archival tape" are, in a sense, oxymorons. These materials have chemicals that will destroy your precious documents over time; furthermore, the very act of attaching a foreign material to your document or photograph will compromise it. You can use these materials to attach photo corners or mount outside envelopes to the pages of a scrapbook or album, but you should never place them directly on the document or photograph you are trying to preserve.

When choosing materials for storing or displaying precious documents, the most important thing to know is what they are made of. You want an inert substance, i.e., one that will not deteriorate, melt, or "bleed" over time, or form noxious chemical interactions with the material they are protecting. While you definitely want "PVC-free" products, buying products labeled as such in discount stores will not necessarily ensure the preservation of your mementos. You are more likely to find reliable products through a specialized archival-material supplier or a photography shop, but even there asking yourself, or the retailer, a few important questions can help ensure that you are getting what you pay for. (See page 124 for a few reliable sources for archival materials.)

PRESERVING THE MEMORIES THEMSELVES

Hearing the stories behind family possessions is often more important than owning the items themselves, and it's also a way to "share the wealth." By eliciting the stories of your family's history from those who know them, and capturing them for the future, many family members can enjoy what's important about an object, even though only one person can actually possess it. Remember, the stories, the recipes, and the music all have more lasting value than the furniture, the pots, and the piano.

As you are putting things aside, packing them, or polishing them up, turn on a tape recorder or set up a video camera and record some family history while you're at it. If those who know the stories aren't there with you at the house, but are still alive, you can take a box of objects, photos, or even a list along on your next visit, and ask them to reminisce about the cast-iron bed, the hand-carved weathervane, the steamer trunk you found in the basement.

If the storyteller needs help getting started, ask open-ended questions like "Where did you get this?" or "What did you bring with you when you came to this country?" If they get bogged down in the story, prompt them gently: "Was this a wedding present?" "And then what happened?" "And where did she end up?" or "Who was that?"

Before everything is removed from the house, you might want to videotape your mother playing her favorite pieces on the piano, perhaps accompanied by your daughter on the clarinet. Or you could record your father making lasagna while he tells his grandchildren about how his mother brought the recipe and the pan with her when she came from

Italy. Tape grandparents, sisters and brothers, aunts and uncles, too, as they talk about their most cherished possessions and their fondest memories. And as you look at family photographs together, keep a tape recorder at hand, so you can capture the stories or reminiscences and use the tape to create an oral family history. These memories, especially when they are recorded, will be a precious gift to yourself and a wonderful legacy for your children.

Smart Questions to Ask

☑ Have we set aside and found a safe place for anything that is important to our family?

☑ Have we made sure that fragile items are properly packed or stored?

☑ If we are putting things into storage, have the boxes or envelopes been clearly marked?

☑ Have family treasures that need to be repaired or restored been placed in temporary safe storage until we can get them to a professional for treatment? Has someone in the family agreed to take on the responsibility for following through with this?

CHAPTER 4

Selling the Goods

AFTER SORTING THROUGH everything in the house and distributing many of the family treasures among yourselves, you may well have found some things that you feel are worth some money. If you want to sell some of them, you have a number of choices. You can have a yard sale to get rid of some of the things, or an auction, or estate sale—two ways of getting rid of everything in the house. You may want to set aside certain items that you feel are of exceptional value and sell them separately—at auction, either on the Internet or through an auction house—or to secondhand retailers. More than likely, you'll use some combination of these sales methods over the course of emptying the house to dispose of items you are not keeping.

YARD SALES

Yard or garage sales (or "stoop sales," as they are called in some urban neighborhoods) are a way to get rid of some, or even most, of the items you no longer want. A yard sale can be a good way of partially emptying out a house at different stages of the process, and can be used in combination with other methods of selling items. It's also a way to start the process: you might want to have a yard sale when you are just starting to get rid of things but not yet ready to empty the house (this is a good way to reduce the amount you will have to deal with ultimately). You could have a sale right after you have sorted through everything and use it to sell those items that you have decided must go. Or you could wait until things have been given to family and friends, donated, or sold, and then use the yard sale as a way of disposing of what's left. Regardless of when you choose to have one, yard sales are a great way to sell items that you definitely want to get rid of. You control what goes out of the house and onto your front lawn, and you keep the crowd outside.

Before you put items from the house into a yard sale, it's important to make it clear to everyone involved which items will be for sale. Decide ahead of time if you will get rid of items that don't sell, or whether you will bring them back into the house for further consideration.

The most successful yard sales are those where the items are priced right—high enough to allow for some bargaining, but low enough to encourage sales. Merchandise should be attractively displayed—with like items shown together, and enough space between displays for people to move around comfortably. Have an extension cord running into the house at hand, so that people can see if appliances work, and include the original instructions or owner's manuals if you have them.

One veteran of yard sales told us you shouldn't take people's sometimes rather insensitive comments personally; people who frequent yard sales are used to bargaining, so don't think of their unwillingness to meet your price as a reflection on your family's taste.

Before You Begin

Check local regulations regarding yard sales. Some towns limit the number of sales you can hold per year, and have rules about where you can sell—on your lawn but not on the sidewalk, for instance. Signs may be regulated too—how big they can be, where they can be posted (not on utility poles or trees, for example), and, just as important, when they have to be taken down.

Weekend days are usually best, but this varies somewhat by neighborhood and season. Think about a backup plan in case of rain, such as staging the sale in your garage or on a covered patio, or announcing an alternate rain date. You can advertise your yard sale by printing flyers with your address and the date of the sale, and posting them around town wherever it is legal to do so. You can also advertise in your local pennysaver newspaper and on the Internet. There are a number of websites that specialize in yard-sale ads, and you might think of posting an announcement on your neighborhood list-serve. On the day of the sale, post signs at nearby intersections directing shoppers to your yard. And before the sale, be sure to have rolls of change and small bills from the bank at hand, so you can make change for customers. A waist pack or an apron with pockets is very handy for holding money, and is safer than keeping it in a box that you may have to walk away from.

NOTE: People shouldn't ask to use your bathroom at a yard sale, but if they do, don't let them. Instead, be prepared to give the person directions to the nearest public restroom.

Pricing

If you are not sure about how to price items, ask a friend who frequents yard sales to help, or visit a couple of yard sales in your area to check out prices. In setting prices, remember to allow room for bargaining by pricing things a bit higher than what you actually want to get. Negotiating is part of the fun of yard sales, so get into the spirit and enjoy it. If several of you are running the sale together, decide ahead of time if all of you will negotiate prices, or if one person will be in charge of that. For collectible items like Barbie dolls or Pez dispensers, check the prices suggested in a collectibles guide before setting your prices. (See page 118.)

You do not have to literally mark each and every item in a yard sale; you can group items. Place books in a carton with the price per book marked on the outside of the carton. Small household items like glasses, teacups, kitchen utensils, and hand towels can be placed on a table, with a piece of paper taped to the table, "50 cents each." Old toys and games can be placed on a blanket on the ground (at kid-level), with a sign that gives the price for each item. You can also help encourage

sales by offering lots: everything in this box for $5.00, or a bag of clothing for $2.00. Larger items should all be priced individually. If you run out of time pricing items, and you have a buyer interested in an item you have no idea how to price, try asking them for an offer. If it seems too low, you can always ask for more, but they may be happy to pay more than you would have dared to ask.

When my father-in-law passed away, my mother-in-law was in her early 70s and in good health, so she took it upon herself to go through a lot of her things. She gathered together everything she wanted to get rid of and she had us and my husband's sister pick out what we wanted. Then she placed an ad in the paper for such things as glassware, tools, etc. With what was left, she had a big garage sale and she was able to get rid of everything. She said she wanted to do that as a gift to us—so that when the time came, we wouldn't have to have the burden of sorting through everything.

ESTATE SALES

Estate sales are the opposite of one-stop shopping—they are "one-stop selling" for all the items in a house, from kitchen towels to the living-room sofa, from plastic drinking glasses to the family car. You would be surprised what people will buy at an estate sale. Mason jars full of buttons, tins full of screws and nails, unused greeting cards and wrapping paper—even laundry detergent and lightbulbs!

How do you know if an estate sale is the right method for you? The great advantage to an estate sale is that in just a couple of days you can empty the house of everything you don't want to keep. Estate sales are usually held over at least two days, often with the prices slashed in half on the final day of the sale. Many buyers will ask about a discount policy, and some will plan to return on the second day to purchase items at a lower price.

Doing It Yourself

If you live in the area and have the time to devote to organizing, displaying, and pricing every item in your family home, and to cleaning up afterward, you may want to handle the sale yourself. You will save the commission paid to professionals and will be able to retain greater control over pricing and other decisions. Even when professional operators are hired to run the sale, there are a lot of decisions that the family has to make. You may decide that in your case it makes more sense to see the whole show through from beginning to end yourself. The following may help you decide.

If you plan to hold the sale yourself, you will have to:

Sort through everything and decide what you and other family members want to keep. Make sure you have all photographs and personal and family memorabilia set aside, and that you have distributed the family heirlooms. Don't underestimate the amount of time this will take. A family home full of twenty-five years' or more worth of accumulated items will take two professionals working together roughly four to five full days to organize, display, and tag. If you're doing this for the first time, it will surely take you longer, especially if you are uncertain of how to price things and become bogged down (understandably) by a variety of emotions during the process.

We had an estate sale after we moved out of our house: there were many items that we simply could not take with us. During the sale, a friend stopped by and saw that a piece of artwork that she had given me as a gift was up for sale. Since I couldn't take it with me, I should have explained that to her and offered it back to her. We're still friends, thank goodness, but had I been more thoughtful we could have avoided an awkward breach in our friendship.

Remove all of the items you want to keep from the house. If this is not possible, you should at least move them to one room in the house and make that room unavailable to browsers. You may want to install a lock to keep shoppers out—just so you don't have to keep repeating that that room is off limits. Remember that at an estate sale, everything that's in view may be purchased, even the mug you had your coffee in that morning. If an item is meaningful, take it out of the house or lock it up. At most estate sales, people feel free to wander into any and every room of the house, looking in drawers and cabinets—even in the medicine cabinet.

Price all items. This is probably the most difficult part of staging a sale yourself. You will have to do some research to find out the going rate for everything from bed linens to dining-room furniture. You will also need to decide whether you're going to negotiate prices. Do you really want to haggle with people over your family's household items? If you are going to drop prices the second day, you may want to hold firm to the prices marked on the first day. On the other hand, you may want to negotiate prices so you can encourage sales and empty the house.

Advertise in your local newspaper, on the Internet, and/or with flyers placed around town. If your house has a lot of items that may be of interest to antiques dealers, you may want to hold the sale during the week, and look into other means of advertising as well.

Be prepared for crowds. Estate sales and antiquing have become very popular hobbies, and both the numbers and the intensity of enthusiasts can be surprising, if not shocking, to the uninitiated. Depending on how much the word is out about what you have to sell, or simply their estate-sale habits, shoppers will line up outside your door the day of the sale for as much as an hour or two ahead of the opening time you've announced. Sometimes they will even come up to the house and peek in the windows. Be ready!

NOTE: Some people ask a nominal admissions fee to estate sales, to discourage the merely curious from taking advantage of the opportunity to snoop. The fee can then be subtracted from the purchasers' total bill of sale.

Be prepared for a variety of mixed emotions—possibly even a roller coaster ride of ups and downs—as you watch familiar family items leave the nest.

Hiring Professionals

When is it a good idea to hire professionals to run the sale? Probably the greatest advantages of hiring professionals are that they know how to price the items and how to attract buyers; but there are others, too. A professionally operated sale will also mean less work for you, and for many people the amount of time involved in setting up an estate sale is difficult to come by. Another advantage to hiring professional estate sales people is that they serve as a buffer between you and some of the more unsavory aspects of running an estate sale. You can be there if you want to, but you can also take a walk when you've heard one too many comments about your mother's appalling taste or snide remarks over the prices you're asking. And finally, they do the clean-up after the sale, a task that can be sad as well as physically tedious.

One antiques dealer who has observed many estate sales is sympathetic to the balancing act required of estate sales conductors. "Often they are trying to meet two goals that may not be entirely compatible," she points out. "There is a need to maximize the value of the estate, but there is also a need to empty the house. Consequently, some compromises may be necessary. Some things may not be sold for as high a price as the family thinks appropriate, but it may be more important that the house be emptied quickly so cleaning can proceed. People need to weigh the pros and cons of the available options, and choose the best option for them; then be content with that choice."

Some of the things sold for more than we would have priced them, and some went for less. I think we made more money in the end by having experts do the pricing than if we had done it ourselves.

If you're planning to hire professionals:

Before you begin, ask a couple of prospective sale operators to come in and evaluate the estate before you start throwing items out or hauling them away. (See page 36.)

Do at least a basic sorting and organizing of items before calling in the professionals, so they can get a realistic sense of what is actually available, and can offer advice about what is best donated or discarded, and what should be saved for the sale. This also gives you the chance to review things item by item.

Separate items you are keeping. Discuss with the professionals how and by when you must isolate any items you are keeping from those that will be offered for sale. Depending on the sale operator's way of doing things, or sometimes depending on available space and logistics, you may be able to lock off a room or two. Or you may have to take everything you're keeping off the premises prior to the operator's coming in to organize the sale. This is important because if it is not clarified and agreed to in writing, you may find yourself being asked to pay a commission on retained items you never intended to go up for sale in the first place.

Be sure the terms of the arrangement are clear. The sale operators should have a standard contract covering the basic points. Some estate sale operators work on a strict commission basis (25 to 30 percent is a reasonable fee). Others may ask for an upfront fee, plus a percentage. Other questions to ask:

- How will the sale be advertised (and how and when is it paid for)?
- Are we allowed to set a minimum price on specific items?
- What becomes of unsold items at the end of the sale? (Does the family retain the right to reclaim some of them if they so desire?)
- Who does the clean-up and/or disposal of items left over that no one wants?
- What kind of accounting is done, and when is payment made to the family?

- What responsibility does the sale operator take for loss, theft, or breakage of valuable objects? (And what precautions will be taken to prevent same?)

Discuss whether or not family members will be present at the sale. In most cases, it is too emotionally difficult for the person whose home is being dismantled to be there, but it's probably good to have at least one representative of the family present, or readily available, to help assure everything goes smoothly, to field any questions that may arise, or to make last-minute decisions that might need to be made. Some estate sale operators, however, will not agree to work this way; they find it too difficult to do their job with family members there.

Trust your instincts when choosing your sale operators. Unless you're really turning the whole thing over to them with no intention of ever looking back, or even being around as they prepare the sale, you want them to be people with whom you have a good rapport. And if you are turning everything over to them, you want them to be trustworthy, honest, professional, and aboveboard in all their dealings. Once you have identified professionals whom you trust and respect, and who respect you, step aside and let them do their job. Try not to hover over them, and second-guess their decisions. Remember, you hired them because they know how to do this, and you don't.

AUCTIONS

It's one of the oldest forms of selling, and it's as modern as eBay. The word *auction* comes from the Latin verb meaning "to increase" and it encapsulates the basic idea that drives this unique and highly effective form of marketing, which pits buyer against buyer in an attempt to bring the greatest possible profit to the seller.

For people emptying out a family home, there are basically three different ways in which auctions can help unload items for a profit.

There are whole-house auctions, sometimes called estate auctions, in which all the contents of the house, and sometimes the house itself, are auctioned away on-site in one day. In many parts of the country, especially in small towns and rural areas, this choice is still the most common method of selling the contents of a home. Very valuable items can also be taken out of the house and sold through another auction venue. Or, depending on the potential value of the contents of the house, some auctioneers may offer to purchase all the goods in the house for a flat fee, or offer the owners a commission on items sold at auction, on consignment.

Whole-house or Estate Auctions

Traditionally, families were expected to do the preparation for whole-house auctions: that is, the sorting, organizing, and hauling out of items for display. Today many auction companies offer families a "full-service" choice, where the auctioneers take over these responsibilities, charging a higher commission than they would if the family were doing all the preparatory work. As in an estate sale, auctioneers work on commission, earning a percentage of total profits on the sale. (Depending on the details of the arrangement, this is usually in the range of 10 to 20 percent.) As with estate sales, placing advertisements and other marketing strategies are the responsibility of the auctioneer, with the cost of the ads being taken out of the family's share of proceeds from the auction. And as in an estate sale, marketing is a key factor in the success of the sale. The amount of lead time is important, as is getting the word out to the right buyers.

Auctions developed a negative connotation in some people's minds during the years of the Great Depression, when many families with no other choice were forced to auction off their worldly goods and often their property. These negative perceptions have lingered in the minds of some to the present day. Indeed, depending on whether or not holding an auction is the right decision, and depending on the nature of

the relationship between the family and the auctioneer, the auction day can be either, as one person we know described it, "the worst day of my life," or an upbeat community-wide social gathering marking the passing from one stage in the life of a family to the next.

A lot depends on the circumstances. Auctions held shortly after the death of a beloved relative can be difficult. As we have said throughout this book, and in a variety of different contexts, you should take as much time as reasonably possible to sort through and dispense with the contents of a home. Decisions made in haste, especially in the wake of a life-altering event such as the death of a spouse or parent, are often regretted. But when the time is right, and all involved parties are ready for such a step, a well-planned and executed auction can be a good and profitable way to dispense with those items in the house that no one in the family wants.

Kristine Fladeboe Duininck was raised in rural Minnesota in her family's auctioneering business. When asked what the advantages might be of holding an auction compared to other means of selling off the contents of a home, she says, "The spirit of competition that drives an auction is just incredible!" While she is passionate about the benefits of holding an auction, she acknowledges that there are some circumstances in which an auction is not the right choice for a family. "In order for an auction to be successful, there has to be a certain number of what we call 'calling cards,'— valuable items that will draw a good crowd," she says. "If all of those items have been taken out of the house already, it's going to be difficult to generate the kind of interest you need in order to make the auction profitable. In a case like that, it probably makes more sense to have a yard sale for what's left over." She recommends that the family call in the auctioneers early in the process, before they start giving things away, or even taking things for themselves. Auctioneers can help the family determine what the "calling cards" in the home are, and this can help them decide what to keep, and what to sell. "An auctioneer should never pressure family members to sell things they really want to keep," Duininck says, "but they can inform the family about what they have that's valuable, and what's not. And that can help them make better decisions, ones that are in the best interests of the whole family, or the estate." Having the auctioneer in on the planning can also help families start talking about things that are difficult to discuss. "Sometimes the auctioneer can help 'crack open' the dynamics in the family, and get people talking about things they need to talk about," she says.

It's important to find the right auctioneer. This means locating someone who has experience in selling the kind of merchandise you have, as well as a good reputation in the community. It's also a question of finding a good match; you want an auctioneer who has the ability to work closely and harmoniously with your family, support you in your decisions, and respect the emotional aspects of the experience. Many states require auctioneers to be licensed; state and regional professional associations, and the National Auctioneer's Association, can provide consumers with advice and assistance in finding qualified auctioneers (see page 121), or you can look for listings in the yellow pages under Auctioneers. You can also ask people in your community for recommendations.

Review the terms of the contract carefully, and ask any questions you may have, the sooner the better. It is especially important to clarify early in the process any items that you do *not* want to sell at the auction, and to refrain from changing your mind once the initial agreement has been set and the process of organizing and sorting is underway. You should also discuss with the auctioneer whether or not any immediate or extended family members wish to participate in the bidding—in some cases this may be acceptable. But if this is the case, the auctioneer will have to make it clear to the crowd that family members bidding are competing on an equal basis with everyone else, and are genuine participants in the sale, so that any perception of attempts to drive prices up can be dispelled.

Selling at a Major Auction House

Selling selected family items at a major auction house is no longer limited to people who own large estates filled with old master paintings. Many houses now have auctions of what they call "affordable home furnishings." This interest in the middle market has been fueled by the popularity of antiques shows on television and on-line auction sites.

You can start by sending high-quality color photographs of the things you'd like to sell to one or more auction houses. Include close-ups of details and any information about any manufacturer's marks, along with a letter giving whatever information you have about the history of the piece. Address the letter to the curator of the department you're interested in—furniture, porcelain, or silver, for example. You can find out the name of the curator by calling the auction house.

If the auction house is interested in selling your item, they will give you an estimated fair market value and propose a "reserve" amount, which is the minimum bid they will accept for the piece. Auction-house charges include insurance, the cost of producing a catalogue photograph, packing and shipping, and, of course, their commission, which is usually from 10 to 20 percent of the final selling price. Your item could sell for the minimum, or it could go for much higher if there are multiple bidders.

If the item does not realize the minimum bid, the auction house may store the piece until the next auction of like items, and will charge you for the cost of storage. Auctions can be held as often as once a month or as seldom as once a year, depending on the kind of items being sold.

On-Line Auctions

Selling items on-line has become so popular that eBay, the largest of the on-line auction sites, has become a part of our vocabulary. There are many on-line auction sites; some of them, like eBay, deal with a wide variety of items; others serve specialized markets such as books, toy-train memorabilia, postcards and other ephemera, historical artifacts, or pottery. Most auction sites have a similar registration requirement and selling process, so the information that follows about eBay is generally applicable to other on-line auction sites as well.

A friend of ours who has a fair amount of experience selling on eBay says that selling on-line entails a learning curve and she has two pieces of advice for the novice. It's best to start by getting advice from someone who has experience selling on-line; and it's a good idea to begin with a less expensive item. Listing a category, coming up with a start price, and factoring in shipping costs are some of the biggest challenges, she says. In addition to consulting with friends and colleagues, there are lots of books available on the subject. (See page 119 for a few titles.)

Before trying to sell anything, be sure you take time to browse the site first, to see how it works. Detailed walk-through tutorials on the site will help answer any questions you may have. Once you are familiar with the general process, you can do more specific research. You can enter the name of an item similar (or identical) to the one you want to sell in the search box on eBay, and then see what comes up and what the current bids are. On the left side of the results page you can click on completed sale. This will show the results for items that have sold in the last two weeks. A look at the sold items will show which ones sold for

Selling On-line

Here's a quick overview of what selling on-line entails. You have to:

- Decide what you want to sell and into which category it fits. (There are more than 1,000 categories on eBay, so this is trickier than it sounds.)

- Complete the registration process, which includes selecting a user name and a password.

- List and describe the items you want to sell. Many sites say adding a photograph taken with a digital camera is helpful, but not necessary; however, you know the saying: "A picture is worth a thousand words." You have a much better chance of selling your item if it is properly photographed.

- Set the terms of the sale and choose a three-, five-, or seven-day auction.

- Respond to questions from potential bidders.

- Monitor daily e-mail updates on the progress of your auction, including the number of bids and the dollar amount. (You will be notified of the high bidder and final price once the auction has ended.)

- Finalize the transaction with the buyer via e-mail.

- Ship the item to the buyer, usually within a few days of receipt of payment, as specified by the site.

- Leave feedback about the buyer and the transaction in the feedback site. This step is important because it helps keep on-line selling honest and allows people to develop confidence in working with others on-line.

the highest price or had the most bids. For these "successful" items you can read how the seller described the piece and in which category it was listed, which will help you in describing and placing your item.

Getting Help from Trading Assistants

It should be clear from the above that while selling on-line offers consumers a convenient new way of unloading secondhand items and making some money doing it, it is also quite time consuming, and requires organizational skills and commitment. It's not an easy answer to emptying out the entire contents of a family home, but help is available from a group of people called trading assistants.

Trading assistants are people who have a great deal of experience in selling on eBay and who saw the entrepreneurial possibilities of setting up what are virtual consignment shops, i.e., selling other people's things on-line. A trading assistant will photograph your item, write the selling description, research and price the item, place it in an appropriate category, monitor the auction, and follow through on the sale—all for a fee plus a percentage of the sale. The use of assistants has become so popular that eBay has begun a formal program for trading assistants, and more than 21,000 people worldwide have registered.

Trading assistants are not difficult to find: some advertise on the Web or in local papers, while others post notices on community bulletin boards. You can also conduct a search in your area by going to "trading assistants" on eBay's website. (Go to the home page, and click on "selling tips." Then click on "Hire someone to sell for you.")

SECONDHAND RETAILERS

Secondhand stores of all kinds are proliferating. That means there are more places to sell your things and greater opportunities to make money. For the best results, check out retailers in advance, and find out what kind of merchandise they offer; then present the items you want to sell in the best possible condition.

There are basically two different kinds of secondhand retailers: *resale shops* buy merchandise outright from individuals (meaning they pay you cash upfront); *consignment shops* accept merchandise on a consignment basis, paying individuals a percentage of the selling price if and when the items are actually sold. Most consignment shops pay you from 40 to 60 percent of the selling price, and often keep the merchandise on display for anywhere from 60 to 90 days. Consignment shops that specialize in clothing usually prefer items that are less than two years old. Before you bring items into a consignment shop, ask about their payment schedule: Will you receive regular updates? How often do they make payments? And do they have any special requirements regarding the types of things they accept?

Some secondhand retailers specialize in vintage items—clothing, accessories, and household goods. There are various definitions of vintage: early (the 1930s and 40s), middle (the 1950s and 60s), and what many of us would consider fairly recent (the 1970s and 80s). Find out what decades the store specializes in so you don't waste your time bringing in things they won't be interested in. Some shops sell clothing only, some sell furniture as well, and some stores have special departments for bridal and prom wear, sporting goods, and music. Check out the types of merchandise they sell, the quality of the items, and the prices they are charging before deciding which resale shop is best for you.

For the best results in selling your items, you should be sure everything you bring in is clean. Clothing should be dry cleaned, on hangers and with the dry cleaning tags attached. Furniture should be dusted and polished. Shoes and handbags should be wiped off and polished. (No one wants to buy anything that is dirty.) If possible, take clothing to the shops in the correct season; spring clothing is most desirable in winter and winter clothing sells best in the fall.

At most consignment shops they will want to look over each piece to decide if they will take it or not. Call ahead to ask how many items they will be willing to look through at one time, and ask if you need an appointment. Resale shops, on the other hand, may be willing to look at whole boxes of clothing and offer a price for the entire box.

To find a shop in your area, look in the yellow pages under Consignment, Resale, or Clothing Bought and Sold.

SELLING DIRECT

For some things, especially large items such as furniture, major appliances, or collections, it pays to sell directly to buyers by placing a classified ad in a local newspaper, or weekly shopping newspaper, or through neighborhood chat-lines or list-serves. You will generally get more money selling this way than you would selling the same item at a yard sale. However, you do have to factor in the cost of the advertisement, and the time and nuisance involved in answering the telephone and showing the items to interested people.

Smart Questions to Ask

☑ Have all involved persons given their consent to sell the objects that are about to go on sale?

☑ Have things that will not be sold been set aside in a safe place? Has it been made clear to whoever will be operating the sale that these things are not to be sold?

☑ If there is to be an auction or estate sale, has someone in the family carefully reviewed the contract and asked any questions that family members may have?

☑ Have we given special consideration to any collections in the house? Has someone done at least a bit of research to make sure that if a collection or collectible items are sold, they are sold in an appropriate way?

Collectibles

The popularity of collecting is undeniable and objects collected range from salt-and-pepper shakers and commemorative plates to lunchboxes and train memorabilia. Here's a look at how to handle collections, whether you have inherited one or have one of your own.

CATALOGING A COLLECTION

If you have a collection, there are several steps you can take to prepare for the inevitable time when someone in your family will be handling it without the benefit of your knowledge. We know of a woman who has a collection of over one thousand aprons, none of it cataloged. Neither of her children has any interest in the collection, and the woman is concerned that no one will appreciate what she has, or the years she spent amassing it. Here are some ways to help your family appreciate what you have, and better the chances that your collection will find a good home.

▶ Make a complete inventory with photographs. With a digital camera or a good 35mm, take a close-up photograph, with proper lighting and background, of each item you have. List all pertinent information: style, color, important characteristics, approximate date of item, date purchased, price paid. The inventory can be created on a computer, typed, or written out longhand. Keep the inventory current—delete items you have sold or traded and add items as you purchase them. Even if you are a casual collector, cataloging what you have will help give it more meaning to others.

▶ If you collect anything that is valuable or unusual, have it insured either with a separate policy or as an addition to your homeowner's policy. To do this, you will need the inventory that you prepared with photographs of the items.

▶ Keep a file of all the receipts for the items you have purchased and a copy of your insurance policy, if you have one. Create a file of newsletter articles and on-line information you have printed out about the items you collect. Make a list of the collectors' clubs or associations you belong to, the meetings or conventions you have attended, and dealers and fellow collectors you have had dealings with, including their telephone numbers and e-mail addresses.

▶ Walk at least one person in your family through your collection; show the person where the inventory is kept, and how your files are arranged. If you have specific bequests for individual items or for the entire collection, let your family know. If you have told your best collector-friend that you would let him or her have first dibs on your collections, tell your family about it.

The best thing to do with a collection, of course, is to enjoy it—share your enthusiasm for it with your family and friends. Cataloging what you have will also help loved ones learn to appreciate your collection, and will help them value it after they have inherited it.

INHERITING A COLLECTION

If you have inherited a collection and need information, a good place to start is with the many collectors' clubs and associations. There are organizations for collectors of everything from postcards to pottery, from teddy bears to teapots, from famous signatures to familiar comic books. From there you can check out newsletters, books, websites, on-line chat groups, and on-line forums for the specific kind of collectible you have.

The best place to sell a collection is probably to a dealer—it is certainly better than breaking up the collection and selling the pieces at a yard sale. Look for a reputable dealer who is knowledgeable in the specific field you need. Ask other collectors for recommendations and check out newsletters and on-line sources. Another option is to sell the collection at a convention of like-minded collectors, but only if you have the time to understand what you have and to check current prices. You could also put the collection up for auction, either at an auction of collectibles or with a nationally known auction house. But remember: in order to realize a good price at auction, there must be people present who know the value of the collection and are willing to bid.

Getting Rid of the Rest

DONATING OR GIVING AWAY household items (finding new homes for them), or recycling them (finding new uses), can be a frustrating and confusing matter. What can you actually give away, and who will take it? This is often the part of the process where people become the most easily bogged down. In this chapter you will find some of the information you need on how get started and how to overcome any logistical complications you may encounter as you begin to deal with those items no one in your family wants.

NOTE: You may want to refer to this chapter both before and after any sale you may hold. If you're hiring experts to operate an estate or moving sale for you, it's best to have them come and take a look at what you have on the premises after you've sorted it all, but before you have actually given anything away. You may want also to consider donating certain things to your local historical society or museum rather than selling them or throwing them away. (See page 94.)

GIVING IT AWAY TO FRIENDS OR FAMILY

In the course of writing this book, we talked to a surprising number of people who decided to give items away, some of them worth quite a bit, rather than either keep or sell them. For many people, the prospect of giving up certain items that are loaded with sentimental importance, or are considered family heirlooms, is just too painful. For these individuals or families, finding an appropriate home for the items becomes more important than making money. One family we know gave an antique cherry wood bedroom set that had been used by their parents and grandparents to a cousin when it was deemed not appropriate for any of the siblings. At the time the decision was being made, this family was told that they were giving away thousands of dollars, but they decided that in the long run, keeping the furniture in the family was more important to them than making money.

Sometimes special items turn up serendipitously. One man we know gave his daughter a set of antique china that he had found, unopened and unused, while cleaning out his father's house. He suggested she could probably get some money for it, but instead she asked him if she could use it, saying she had never had anything that nice before. The father was "just happy it had a good home."

Sometimes, for a variety of reasons, people may decide that holding a sale is not for them, and that they prefer to just give things away. "We didn't have any kind of sale," one woman told us. "I know we could have probably gotten some money from some of the old china and pottery that we just let go. But we didn't want anyone traipsing through our house, and we didn't want anyone to know the house was going to be empty. We ended up letting the mover, who had helped us so much in the process, just take it all away." This decision was right for that family, and this woman was comfortable with her decision. "Even though I know we gave away things that were valuable, I don't regret it," she concluded.

DONATING AND RECYCLING

When people want to donate household items, often the first place they think of is one of the major charities like Goodwill, the Salvation Army, or Big Brothers/ Big Sisters of America—and for good reason. These agencies are willing to take many of the things we would like to get rid of and put them to good use by either giving them to the needy or selling them in their thrift shops, with the profits going to support their social services programs. Often these organizations will make it even easier on donors by coming to the home to pick up donated items. And when you give to charitable organizations, your donation is tax deductible.

To be considerate when donating, make sure that all clothes are clean and wearable, all appliances are in working order, and anything with multiple pieces, like children's games or tool sets, have all the parts intact. Exactly which items charities accept varies from organization to organization and from location to location, so it's best to contact your local outlet for specifics. (See page 125.)

Some charities post guidelines on their websites for items they will accept. Most charities accept clothing of all types, and shoes for men, women, and children, as well as costume jewelry and accessories; appliances in working order and household items; televisions, stereos, and computers; books, toys and games, and sporting goods. Most do not accept broken appliances, water beds, furniture in bad repair, magazines or old encyclopedias, bathroom fixtures such as toilets or sinks; tires, paint, swing sets, water heaters, windows, or doors.

Household items can also be donated to smaller or locally based charities, such as veterans' associations, churches and synagogues, children's charities, and programs for the elderly. Community theaters, women's shelters, prisons, hospitals, rehabilitation centers, and nursing homes also often accept donations of furniture and household goods. You might also inquire at local schools, preschools, day-care centers, art schools, and after-school programs run by schools, churches, or the YMCA or YMHA, to see if they could use toys, games, books, desks, art supplies, or musical instruments.

The following are suggestions and tips for donating various types of household items. For a list of charities and companies that accept donations, and information on what specifically they accept, see the Donation and Recycling Directory on pages 125–130.

Furniture

Most of the major charities accept donations of furniture. You can also ask organizations that help set up apartments for the poor or homeless in your community if they would like the furniture. A religious or charitable organization that is setting up a local community center may be interested in living room, kitchen, or den furniture. (Some smaller organizations do not have the resources to pick up large items and may ask that you deliver the furniture to them.)

Clothing

Where does it come from? Clothing does accumulate, sometimes so much that it almost seems to multiply on its own. Business clothing—suits for women and men in good condition—can be donated to organizations that outfit people who are going on a job interview for the first time. To donate this type of clothing, make sure it is clean and on hangers, if possible. Casual wear can go to thrift shops, women's shelters, or local organizations that help the homeless or the poor, disabled, or otherwise needy in your community. Organizations in several cities now accept prom dresses and give them to young girls who could not otherwise afford a gown. Unusual or vintage clothing and accessories may be appreciated by your local community theater or your high-school or college theater group. Hats, dress shoes, and other accessories may be welcome at a preschool or kindergarten for their dress-up corner.

Computers

If it's true that by the time you get your computer out of the box and installed, it is already outdated, then any computer that has been sitting around for a while is certainly of questionable value. But that doesn't mean it can't have another life, either intact or as parts.

Some organizations will only accept a computer with a Pentium processor and with a functioning keyboard, mouse, monitor, and modem or network card. Most schools need computers that are less than two years old if they are to be used in the classroom. However, an old computer that still works might be welcomed by a religious or community group to keep its membership list, or to print out bulletins and newsletters; and a high-school student with meager resources might love to have a computer to type up school reports, even if he cannot log onto the Internet. If the computer has children's software, a preschool in a poor neighborhood may be able to use it.

According to a National Recycling Coalition report, 20 million computers became obsolete in 1998, but only 11 percent were recycled. This means that all the others are either needlessly taking up space in homes and businesses, or are in landfills, where they are disintegrating into various forms of toxic waste. To encourage the recycling of computers, some manufacturers and many charitable organizations have set up programs for taking back equipment and either refurbishing it or using it for parts. With everyone working together, electronic equipment and the toxic waste it creates can be kept out of our landfills and may even be put to good use.

NOTE: Be sure to remove all personal files before you donate a computer. To do this, you need a utility software that erases all information from the hard drive. (Putting files in the icon marked "trash" removes them from the desktop but not from the hard drive.)

Cell Phones

Cell phones are tiny, but there's nothing little about the problem of disposing of them. Old cell phones should not end up in landfills; but one study estimates that by the year 2005, there will be 500 million stockpiled used cell phones, weighing over 250,000 tons, that could potentially end up in our waste system. Fortunately, a number of

Caveat Donor!

Some national charitable organizations used to keep donation bins in parking lots or on street corners, but stopped using them because they were often filled with trash as well as with usable clothing. New, brightly colored drop boxes have begun to appear in many cities; the company that owns these bins is a for-profit company that sells the clothing overseas, where there is a huge market for secondhand clothing. Many people assume that things left in these boxes are being donated to a charity (and the only clue that they are not is the ".com" that follows the Web address listed on the boxes). You may choose to use these drop boxes to donate your used clothing because they are convenient, but if you do, you should be aware of two things: when you do this, you cannot get a receipt for tax purposes because you are not making a charitable donation; and nonprofits have to report where their money goes, while private companies do not.

How much of a tax deduction can you claim for donating an old car to charity? According to the General Accounting Office, the investigative arm of Congress, much more than the charity will actually receive. You can claim the fair market value of the car, which you can determine using a source such as the Kelley Blue Book or Edmunds.com, which factors in the mileage and condition of the car. (Make sure to take a photo of the car to verify the condition.) The charity often pays for the towing or delivery of the car, cleaning and repairs, and advertising, then hires a professional fund-raiser to auction the car. All of these expenses are deducted from the amount realized at the auction, resulting in the charity netting a small fraction of the amount the owner is allowed to claim. Knowing this, you may still choose to donate your car. If you do, remember that it is your responsibility to transfer ownership. And the IRS requires a professional appraisal for deductions over $5,000.

It May Not Be Junk

What's "junk" to some people is a valuable historical record to others. Mona Nelson, executive director of Minnesota's Kandiyohi County Historical Society, agrees: "Often some of the first things to go into the Dumpster can be enormously valuable to state or local historical societies. For example, ephemera—things like old cards, letters, photographs, and maps—these things can tell us a lot about our social history." Printed announcements, invitations, ticket stubs, personal diaries, scrapbooks full of old newspaper clippings, old yearbooks, advertising buttons or signs, and product packaging are also the kinds of items that a local historical society may be interested in.

And it's not only the museums that may want these documents: a friend of ours was dismayed to learn that her Italian grandparents' immigration papers were tossed into the garbage by an aunt who saw no value in keeping them any longer. If you find letters in your home that were written by people who are still alive, they may appreciate getting them back at this time for an unexpected peek at their past. If no one in your family wants these kinds of things, you might think about approaching museums, libraries, or local historical societies with them. One national nonprofit organization is dedicated to collecting, preserving, and creating a national archive of old war letters. (See page 129.)

On the other hand, there is paperwork that you will no doubt want to get rid of, and some of it may contain information that you don't want to leave in the garbage. Old credit-card statements, tax forms, pay stubs, and the like should either be burned or shredded to prevent private and confidential information from leaking out to places or people you don't want to have it. But just remember that these are nonreversible activities—so don't go too fast, and do be highly conscious of what you're getting rid of.

organizations have programs for recycling the phones or giving them to victims of domestic violence or children's support services. Most organizations that collect the phones ask that you include the battery, charger, and instructional booklet if you have them.

Medical Supplies

Unfortunately, expensive as they are, medical supplies are difficult to donate. Hospitals and nursing homes often cannot accept such donations from individuals for reasons of liability. However, there are organizations that collect medical supplies and equipment from individuals to give to doctors who volunteer in developing countries. These organizations will accept supplies, equipment, and instruments, but not medicines or pharmaceuticals. Some organizations also collect specific items such as eyeglasses, hearing aids, crutches, wheelchairs, and prostheses.

Books

It would be nice if every neighborhood had a tradition of recycling books, like some in New York City, where residents often leave used books stacked on their front steps or on the sidewalk as giveaways for anyone walking by. But there are many places to donate books. Local libraries, church or synagogue libraries, hospitals, rehabilitation centers, and nursing homes all appreciate book donations. Children's books are often welcome at after-school programs or in women's shelters. Some public schools collect books to help set up classroom libraries in poorer school districts; check to see if your local school participates in such a program. Or call a school principal in an area you think would benefit from such a gift to ask about making a direct donation—of children's books to an elementary school or classic works of literature to a high school. Prisons often welcome donations of textbooks. Yearbooks may be useful to genealogical groups, and books about local areas may be of interest to the historical society or local museum.

Odds and Ends

Fabric, yarn, beads and other costume jewelry, wood, leftover tile, paint, even broken pottery can be transformed into works of art when donated to schools or community centers. Depending on the material, you can donate these items to preschools, after-school programs, community centers, programs for seniors, or community college art departments. These places will also welcome traditional art supplies such as paint, brushes, canvas, and clay.

THROWING OUT THE TRASH

Whether you are sorting through one closet at a time or emptying the whole house in a week, after you have taken what you want and donated the rest, you will have to dispose of the trash. If the amount of trash is manageable, at the end of each day you can put it into large trash bags, tie them securely, and leave them at the curb or in the alley with the regular trash. Call the local sanitation department first to verify the size of the containers or nature of the articles that can be left curbside, and which days are scheduled for garbage pick up.

If you are disposing of large amounts of trash, you may need to rent a Dumpster. Check the yellow pages of the telephone book under Rubbish or Rubbish Disposal to find companies that rent Dumpsters. Dumpsters come in various sizes, so be sure to ask what your options are before ordering. Depending on how bulky the items are, you may want to hire a company that brings a Dumpster and hauls the trash out of the house for you. Some companies also have compactors for the trash.

If you are disposing of large appliances—freezers, refrigerators, water coolers, dehumidifiers, air conditioners, or any type of appliance containing Chlorofluorocarbon (CFC) gas (also known as Freon), call the sanitation department to ask about the proper disposal procedure. If you are permitted to leave the appliance on the curb for pick up, by law you must remove the doors of refrigerators and freezers for safety reasons.

One nationwide company specializes in picking up whole houses full of stuff people don't want. Several workers come with a truck and boxes, empty everything from the house, pack it up, and take it away, and then donate or sell the usable items. This is a service that you pay for: whatever profit may be had in resale of items hauled away goes to the company, not to the family.

Hazardous Waste

As you clean out under the sink, from the medicine cabinet, the basement, and the garage, you will be faced with many items that are toxic to the environment. These include (but are by no means limited to) household cleaners and chemicals, aerosol cans, batteries, pesticides (including ant and roach killers, flea collars and sprays), mothballs, metal polish, paint (both oil and latex), swimming-pool chemicals, medicines, gasoline, antifreeze, and motor oil. Check the expiration dates on items such as household cleaners, paint, and charcoal; you can offer still usable items to neighbors or friends or sell them at your estate sale or auction.

To dispose of the rest, first read the packaging for the preferred method of disposal. *Never pour anything down the sink or into the toilet unless the manufacturer says that this is the best way to dispose of it.*

Always wear work gloves when handling toxic materials, especially if they are old and have been stored under the sink or in the basement for a long period of time. (Chemical reactions may have happened over time and the containers may not be as stable as they once were.) Always keep children away from toxic materials. And never put several different kinds of household chemicals into the same container for disposal; you don't know how they may react together.

To find your local solid waste agency, look in the government section of your telephone book under headings for Solid Waste, Public Works, Garbage, Trash, or Refuse. Then ask the agency or department which items are recyclable and where they can be dropped off, and where special-waste drop-off sites are located. Or check on-line resources for recycling waste. (See page 130.) State and local laws may be stricter than the federal requirements printed on packaging, so always check with local agencies.

It may be tempting, especially if you are pressed for time, to just throw all these materials into a plastic bag and put them out with the regular trash. You may think that you are not likely to get caught. However, this is not only illegal in many areas, it's also not socially responsible or fair. When toxic materials end up in our landfills, they poison the earth and the water we drink. This destroys the environment and creates unnecessary health risks for the current as well as future generations. If you don't want to deal with the nuisance of this level of cleaning detail yourself, there are cleaning services who will properly dispose of these materials for you.

Smart Questions to Ask

☑ Has everyone involved in the process given his or her consent to getting rid of the things that are being given away, donated, or thrown away?

☑ Has someone carefully checked through everything that is going out of the house to make sure nothing important is lost?

☑ Do we, or does the estate, need a tax receipt for things that are being donated? If so, have we made arrangements to get itemized receipts?

☑ Has someone checked local safety and environmental regulations before throwing out toxic waste?

Lessons Learned

THE EXPERIENCE OF EMPTYING a home is a unique one for every family, and for every individual within each family. And though there is no one right way of doing it, as we talked to people in the process of putting this book together, a few common "lessons learned" came up over and over again. Some of the lessons apply directly to the emotional experience and actual process of emptying a house: others, more general and practical in nature, can be applied to living our everyday lives in such a way that when the time comes to empty the next house, it does not have to be quite as overwhelming for everyone involved as it might have been. These lessons learned fall into a few main categories.

TAKE YOUR TIME

The one thing almost everyone we spoke to emphasized is that this is a huge task. Rushing through it is one of the best ways to end up with regrets, so try to allow plenty of time.

How much time is enough? Well, that's impossible to say because it's different for every family, and a lot depends on your unique situation. We've talked to some families who did the bulk of it in a few days, and others who took as long as five years to complete the process. In one sense, doing it right can take a lifetime; some of the suggestions in this chapter will help you form habits now that can make the inevitable emptying-out easier, even if that day is years ahead. But whether you are in the process now or are preparing to do it later, there are ways to make the experience more or less enjoyable, so you can walk away at the end of it all feeling you've done things "right," or at least as well as you could.

If you possibly can afford to, take your time and don't try to do it all too fast. Also, don't give away too much too soon. In the anxiety of moving there's a tendency to think, "I'm never going to use that again," or "I don't want that anymore." Then you get into your new place, and there's an empty shelf, and you think, "Now why did I give that away?"

COMMUNICATE!

For many, perhaps most people, the desire to maintain family harmony throughout this process is more important than anything else. And while we certainly agree that maintaining family harmony is more important than acquiring things for oneself, we also think it's important that everyone

Avoiding Common Regrets

These are a few of the most commonly expressed regrets, gathered from the people we spoke to:

- Threw out, or gave away, things I now wish I had.
- Sold something valuable for too little.
- Gave away items my siblings later wanted.
- Broke or lost valuable or special things in the process of emptying the house.
- Stored for too long items I ended up throwing out or giving away.
- Kept things I didn't really want or need just because they belonged to my parents.

involved feels safe and secure in expressing their feelings and free to make their wishes known. Unfortunately, sometimes the fear of upsetting others, or unleashing old arguments, keeps families from having the kind of free and open (yet respectful) dialogue that is needed to ensure that everyone ends up feeling as if they've had their say and been heard. Taking your time helps ensure that these important conversations can take place. So does creating an atmosphere in which every person involved is encouraged to speak their mind, with plenty of room for give and take, and with the understanding that everyone is different and has their own set of feelings to deal with. All of this will help to leave little room for future resentments.

$\mathcal{I}$ have seen friends and members of my own family live with the anger, resentment, or regret that came about as a result of never confronting someone who acted in a selfish way regarding an estate's contents. Maybe there's no good way to deal with such people. But maybe their grief is just coming out sideways in an awkward, inappropriate way. Maybe calling them on their behavior could resolve tension and prevent years of future resentment. And even if it can't, maybe the confrontation, no matter how upsetting at the time, wouldn't be nearly as hard as carrying the burden of the anger and regret over failing to speak one's mind.

ENJOY THE PROCESS

Throughout this book, we've talked about various ways you can have fun while you empty out the house—invite extended family to come and help, order in food and take breaks, take time to watch old movies together, and reminisce together while you sort through the mountains of objects. And while you're at it, don't forget that the good memories are not all in the past—the process of emptying out the house can become a happy family memory for you and your children. They're watching, they're listening, they're taking notes on how families work and play together. Take pictures: of your favorite niece twirling around the room in your old Easter dress; of you and your siblings gathered on the front porch for the last time, posed in the identical positions of a favorite old family snapshot; or of several generations seated together on the living room couch before the room is dismantled.

Every house that has been lived in and enjoyed deserves to have a proper final fling. So, say a joyful farewell! Whether it's an 80th birthday celebration, a moving-out party to say goodbye to the neighbors, or just a congenial and relaxed family get-together after a funeral is over, make sure that you and your family have one last happy gathering to remember, so that when you take that last walk through the halls, one of the sounds you will hear echoing in your mind is that of recent laughter.

Our daughters came back and had a big party before we left the house for good. They invited all their old friends, or any of them who were close enough to be able to come. This helped them to achieve closure.

Saying Goodbye, and Moving On

When you're emptying a home, it sometimes seems like an endless process. But eventually, the moment you never thought would arrive comes, and you—or someone in your family—take a final walk through the empty halls, and close the door. Now what? Some people are just happy that it's over, and relieved that a chapter in their lives is finished: others are left with lingering feelings of sadness. Whatever your emotions are, acknowledge them, at least to yourself, and talk about them with others if that helps. Then move on!

- "Even though I knew we had to sell it, I felt devastated at losing my childhood home. I couldn't believe I would never go back to that house! It took a while to get over that feeling."

- "Your possessions create your home—the house is simply a box. When you remove those possessions, you are stripping away your home, your security, your comfort zone. You have to have faith that these things will return when you are ready to create the new environment, and that it will be just as secure as the old one was."

- "In some ways, I think it's a good thing that there is so much physical drudgery and tediousness involved. It keeps you from dwelling too much on the fact that you are saying goodbye to the place that was the setting for so many important moments in your life. If I had had more time there, I think it would have been very important to break away from it all periodically, to take long walks, or go to a movie. Something, anything to interrupt the intensity of it."

- "It's like childbirth—once it's over, you forget about the misery. You get over it!"

Let Go

It's not unusual to experience a potent mixture of unsettled emotions in the immediate aftermath of this process. If you are closing up a home that has been in your family for many years, especially if that home is the last physical link to a part of the world that is dear to you, you're likely to feel at the very least a tender nostalgia, and perhaps even a profound sense of loss or regret. Even if the decision to let that home go was one that you know was right, the actual letting go can be difficult. For many people, feeling this sadness is a perfectly natural part of the process; go ahead and allow yourself to feel momentarily sad, or nostalgic. Then take the next big step, and move on. The rest of your life is about to begin!

Throw As You Go

The practical lessons learned may help make the process a little easier for you or your children when the time comes to empty the next house. The best way to avoid having to sort through tons of accumulated family stuff, of course, is not to let it accumulate in the first place. Make a habit of regularly weeding out unnecessary items. Go through closets and drawers to get rid of clothes that are no longer worn, kitchen utensils that are no longer used, books that are no longer read, and give these items away. You will enjoy the additional space and will be gratified that someone who needs the items will be able to enjoy them. When it's time to empty the house, the fewer the number of things to sort through, the less overwhelming the task will be. If you need help doing this, there are many useful books on getting organized (see page 120) or you may want to consult a professional organizer (see page 123).

Of course, we all know that for most people this is much easier said than done. Here are some suggestions for dealing with specific categories of things that seem to multiply before your eyes.

Children's Artwork

You'll want to live with your children's artistic creations before you think about disposing of them. Displaying your children's artwork is good for their developing egos, makes for a cheery and bright home, and may actually make it easier to let them go eventually, knowing you've fully enjoyed them along the way.

- Designate a particular wall or area of your house to display the work as it is being created. Even in small spaces, there are ways to do this: one of us used the wall behind our children's beds, and covered it from floor to ceiling with our kids' artwork; an acquaintance used the wall between the kitchen and the dining room. Put the date, the name of the artist, and any relevant comments or background information ("This is Grandma's flower garden") on the back of the work. From time to time, take photos of the display for your archives. Change the artwork as often—or as seldom—as your child wants.

- Find ways to use or recycle the artwork. Drawings on large pieces of newsprint can be used as wrapping paper (if your child agrees); smaller pieces can be folded in half and used as greeting cards.

- Photograph your child's work, especially the three-dimensional pieces, which are difficult to keep, so you have a record of it.

- At the end of each school year, create a system for saving some of the work. You can decide ahead of time that you will choose a certain number of pieces—say six or ten—or you can designate a box or artist's portfolio for safekeeping and allow your child to save anything that fits in the box. The important thing is to regularly select items to save, because you just can't keep it all.

- When you do throw the work out, especially the work of very young children, don't let them see you do it. As they get older, they will understand the need to select only certain items to save, and they can help you do it. But when they're young, they should not have to observe their work being thrown away. That's confusing and painful!

$\mathcal{W}$e visited my grandmother in a nursing home often when my older daughter was in nursery school. Always a prolific artist, she would bring along a piece of her art, 'To Great Grandma,' written on it, as a gift. The art brightened my grandmother's day as well as her room, and gave the staff something to talk to her about long after our visit. It also created a beautiful bond between my daughter and her great-grandmother.

Children's Schoolwork

Some parents save everything; others throw everything out. We think there's a happy medium somewhere between the two.

One way to sort through schoolwork is to separate the creative work—essays, book reports, journals—from worksheets and tests. You might want to save a perfect spelling or math test, but reading your child's original work will give you the most pleasure in years to come. You may also want to save a test or homework assignment that has a particularly relevant—or amusing—comment from the teacher.

We know of one parent who saved all of the science projects and social studies posters for all three of her children. They are all grown now, with families of their own, and their work is still sitting in their parent's attic. As an alternative to saving all the actual projects, you might photograph your child in front of them and label the photos, along with any descriptive information or special memories of making the project. Then toss out the work itself.

It may be easier for the child if you sort and toss out items at the beginning of the next school year rather than at the end of the current year. The excitement about a new year will help distance the child from the work of the previous year and may lessen any emotional attachment to it.

Photographs

Keep only the best ones. Toss photos that are out of focus, dark, or otherwise unsatisfactory. The best ones are not necessarily the posed pictures. They may be the ones where someone is making a funny face, or people are participating in favorite activities—playing ball, gardening, or snuggling up with the dog.

Share the photos with family and friends. If you have several shots of your child and her best friend, give the friend a photo or two. Grandparents always love to receive photos, but so will cousins and aunts and uncles.

Books

If you love to read, you are almost certain to be familiar with the problem of having too many books in the house. There's probably nothing you can collect that has such a bad resale value, nor such a rich intellectual one. So go ahead and enjoy the habit, but if you are a book buyer, you should develop some kind of system for purging your shelves regularly.

At least once a year, go through your bookshelves and ask your children to do the same. Make sorting through your books a regular family activity, perhaps as part of spring cleaning or in the early fall before the start of the school year, and decide together what you will do with the books you no longer wish to keep.

Clothing

Professional organizers advise tossing out any clothing that hasn't been worn in the last year. This is good advice. Twice a year, go through your closets and pull out anything that doesn't fit, isn't in style, or that you don't like, and donate the clothing.

If you are saving children's clothing for a younger child, keep only items in good condition. Put them in a box labeled with the size and season. You can keep a few favorite but outgrown items of clothing, like a team jersey or a party dress, but limit it to one or, at most, two items per child per year; store them in a well-labeled box. (See page 58 for more on saving textiles.) If your family no longer needs the clothes, give them away to a children's shelter, a church or synagogue group, or any organization that will see that the clothing goes to those in need, or sell them to a consignment shop.

One exception to the "throw as they grow" edict for children's clothing is to save anything that is handmade—knitted sweaters and hats, hand-embroidered dresses, and the like. You may want to save those for your children's children.

Toys

Once or twice a year, ask your children to go through their toys. Give the ones they no longer play with to younger children you know or to children's shelters, or sell them at a flea market table at a school, church, or synagogue fundraising event. You can put away one or two favorites for a memory box, but try to be ruthless about the others.

Do keep board games, jigsaw puzzles, and any other activities that can be enjoyed by family members of all ages. Also, keep a small basket of toys for infants and toddlers, to have handy when families with

babies or small children come to visit. These toys will be appreciated by both the visiting parents and children, and will make your home a welcoming place for families with young children to visit.

THINK AHEAD

If you form consistent and efficient habits of getting rid of the junk and just plain excess cluttering up your life, you will have more time and space to devote to preserving and organizing the important things.

Photographs

Label all photographs on the back with names, dates, and any other significant information (location if known, the occasion, any other helpful details), using a soft (#2) lead pencil, and writing softly (to avoid damaging the photograph), and clearly. (You can get pencils specially made for this purpose from photography suppliers.) Of course *now* you know the name of your child's best friend, the one who is sitting next to him in the second-grade class photo. But if the friend moves away, or you do, it's likely that by the time your child graduates from high school you won't remember it anymore. When they're older, your children will be gratified to have details like this preserved.

Do the same with old family pictures: *you* know that the people in the photograph of your sister's wedding are Great-aunt Ida's children, that the year Dad's bowling team placed first was 1963, that the ski vacation was in New Hampshire, but your children probably will not. (Use first and last names, rather than "Aunt Ida" or "Grandpa," so that anyone reading the label in the future will know who the person was, even if they don't know who labeled the photograph.) If you don't end up keeping the photos in your family, they will be more valuable to local historical societies and museums if they are labeled. In fact, many historical societies and libraries will not accept unlabeled photographs unless they are of clearly identifiable local landmarks or people.

If keeping up-to-date photo albums for each of your children seems too hard to do, keep the photos in separate boxes labeled with each child's name and the inclusive dates of the photos. This way each child will have a box of childhood photos to take to his own home when he has one. If you have a digital camera, you can create a photo disk or CD for each child, labeled with the child's name and the dates of the photos. The same family photos can be put on each CD, along with each child's individual school activities and after-school events.

Remember all those home movies "trapped" in an obsolete technology? Don't let your kids have to deal with the same frustration: keep your photographic images, whether still or moving, digital or not, organized and up to date, and transfer images from old formats to new ones as technologies evolve. If you don't have the time, patience, or the expertise to do it yourself, you can take it to professionals who will do it for you. This is money well spent.

Ask your photo processor what kind of paper is being used to print your photographs: Fujichrome Crystal Archive paper has a very good reputation, and even many drugstore and chain retail photo processing units now use it.

Know that any image that is displayed will fade. If it's a picture you have chosen to hang on the wall or keep on your desk, it's probably one you like a lot. So display copies, but always keep the originals in a safe place, away from light, heat, and excess moisture.

Videotape

In addition to the dangers that affect other media—heat, light, moisture, insects, and other pests—the very act of playing back videotape is harmful to the tape, even if it stored as it should be, is always played in a clean VCR playback device, and is never left in the machine overnight. (If the video collection in your home does not fit this description, don't worry. You are not alone.)

How can you safeguard precious memories stored on videotape? For starters, use high-quality, brand-name videotapes, record at the standard level, and remember to punch the tabs out so it can't be accidentally recorded over. Be sure to always keep at least two copies of any important tape—one "playback" copy, and one for storage. The storage copy should be kept away from heat, light, dust, and moisture, and kept in a vertical position. (Once a year, storage copies should be checked to see if they are still playable.) And video that is ten years old or more should be transferred either to new videotape or to another storage medium. (Keep the original, since each reformatting will result in some lost resolution.)

Finally, following a few basic rules for safe handling of videotape will go a long way toward keeping a fragile medium in good condition. Don't drop or throw tapes; don't force them into the machine; never touch the surface of the tape with bare hands; keep your machine clean; and always rewind tapes, preferably at a low speed.

Important Documents

Keep your most important records—birth, death, marriage, and divorce certificates; immunization records, social security cards, passports, naturalization papers, military service registration or discharge papers, wills, insurance policies, and other important financial records—in a fire-safe box in a central, easily accessed location. Documentation that is important for sentimental reasons or helpful for future family historians—birth announcements, invitations to and programs from christenings, bar and bat mitzvahs, weddings, and funerals; report cards and diplomas; letters, diaries, journals, resumes; newspaper announcements of birth, death, marriage, promotions, and retirement—should be kept separately, preferably in archival-quality storage containers, and organized as well as you can manage. And make sure your children know where these things are kept.

ONE FINAL WORD

Having emptied our own family homes of decades' worth of accumulated stuff, we are well aware of how much work it entails and what an emotional roller coaster it can be. In talking with many other people, our understanding of some of the things we experienced and observed during this process was confirmed. Perhaps the most fundamental thing is that there are basically two kinds of people when it comes to cleaning out a house. There are "the throwers," who relish the experience of clearing out and moving on, and who will empty a house quickly and efficiently. And there are "the keepers," who will be compelled to preserve special things as well as memories, and who will linger over the process. In order to successfully empty a house full of memories you need people who can balance these two attributes, and can call on each of them when it is appropriate. These are people who have come to the realization that the most valuable thing in a house is the life that has been lived there.

And Another Thing...

As we worked on this book, we got a lot of advice from people who had been through the process of emptying a home. What we learned from all of this can be boiled down to what most of us learned in kindergarten—or should have learned, anyway.

▶ **Think before you act.** "The first step is to think it all through—think, think, think—before you do so much as to call the movers."

▶ **Be considerate of others' feelings.** "Family members should be sensitive to one another and recognize that we grieve in different ways and at different speeds, and will therefore respond to the task with a wide range of emotions. I would also hope that rather than jumping into the house-cleaning task with a vengeance, they would begin by discussing and agreeing how the task should proceed."

▶ **Take your time.** "The old saying about not making major decisions or changes at times of emotional stress is good advice. You can always get rid of something later, but you can't retrieve something hastily discarded."

▶ **Things worth doing are worth doing well.** "My sister and I took a long time—more than a year—to go through all the things in my mom's house, and we did it in incremental stages. We started by going through her clothing, and my dad's, which was still there eight years after he had died. We started a few days after her funeral, when we were both there. Then we got together there every few months, and would go through another layer of the things in the house. Some of the things that we knew would be more difficult to decide about, like her jewelry, we left for later, and if we both wanted the same thing we just deferred the decision. As time passed, we were both able to give and take, and it all worked out. I think it was better doing it that way, with time between rounds."

▶ **Share with others.** "As you go about dividing up things, if and when they start to get heated, remember to step back from the process and remind your

self that these are all just things. You didn't need them before, and you don't need them now. It's not worth fighting over them."

▶ **Appreciate your family.** "We waited to empty my mother-in-law's house until after she was settled in the nursing home, but I think we waited too long. We had ample time to go through the house at a leisurely pace, but by that time she was no longer able to communicate. I'm sure there were stories to go along with a lot of the 'junk' we were sifting through, but there was no one to tell us the stories. I guess the ideal situation would be to have the owners of the house there when things are being sorted."

▶ **Keep your priorities straight.** "No matter how often I was reminded, or reminded myself, that what we were dealing with was just 'stuff,' I found it very difficult to divorce myself from all the meaning and the memories attached to that 'stuff.' It's important to keep telling yourself that what you are working with is just things—and that what's important is your life, not the things in it."

▶ **Good work is deeply rewarding.** "I didn't dread the process before it began, but I did view it as an obligation, something I simply was going to have to do. But during, and afterward, I was surprised at the many small and unexpected joys it contained. I learned that cleaning out a parent's house doesn't have to be a chore; it can be the beginning of healing the grief you feel over your loss."

Helpful Books and Websites

CHAPTER ONE

First Things First

Barney, Colleen and Victoria F. Collins. *Best Intentions: Ensuring Your Estate Plan Delivers Both Wealth and Wisdom.* Chicago: Dearborn Trade Publishing, 2002.

Morris, Virginia. *Caring for Aging Parents.* New York: Workman Publishing, 1996.

Morris, Virginia. *Talking About Death Won't Kill You.* New York: Workman Publishing, 2001.

Stum, Marlene S. *Who Gets Grandma's Yellow Pie Plate? A Guide to Passing on Personal Possessions.* St. Paul: University of Minnesota Extension Service, 1999. (There is also a website: www.yellowpieplate.umn.edu, and a video to help get families talking. For information call 800-876-8636 or e-mail: order@extension.umn.edu.)

CHAPTER TWO

Sorting It Out

Kovel, Ralph and Terry Kovel. *Kovels' Antiques and Collectibles Price List 2003.* New York: Three Rivers Press, 2002.

Prisant, Carol. *Antiques Roadshow Collectibles: The Complete Guide to Collecting 20th Century Toys, Glassware, Costume Jewelry, Memorabilia, Ceramics, and More.* New York: Workman Publishing, 2003.

Prisant, Carol. *Antiques Roadshow Primer: The Introductory Guide to Antiques and Collectibles from the Most–Watched Series on PBS.* New York: Workman Publishing, 1999.

Rosson, Joe. L. and Helaine Fendelman. *Price It Yourself! The Definitive, Down-to-Earth Guide to Appraising Antiques and Collectibles in Your Home, at Auctions, Estate Sales, Shops, and Yard Sales.* New York: HarperResource, 2003.

Rosson, Joe. L. and Helaine Fendelman. *Treasures in Your Attic: An Entertaining, Informative, Down-to-Earth Guide to a Wide Range of Collectibles and Antiques from the Hosts of the Popular PBS Show.* New York: HarperResource, 2001.

CHAPTER THREE

Saving Precious Memories

Long, Jane S. and Richard W. *Caring for Your Family Treasures: A Concise Guide to Caring for Your Cherished Belongings.* New York: Harry N. Abrams, 2000.

Mailand, Harold F. and Dorothy Stites Alig. *Preserving Textiles: A Guide for the Non-Specialist.* Indianapolis Museum of Art, 1999.

Schultz, Arthur W. *Caring for Your Collections: Preserving and Protecting Your Art and Other Collectibles.* New York: Harry N. Abrams, 1992.

Sturdevant, Katherine Scott. *Organizing and Preserving Your Heirloom Documents.* Cincinnati: Betterway Publications, 2002.

Taylor, Maureen A. *Preserving Your Family Photographs: How to Organize, Present and Restore Your Precious Family Images.* Cincinnati: Betterway Publications, 2001.

Wilhelm, Henry. *The Permanence and Care of Color Photographs: Traditional and Digital Color Prints, Color Negatives, Slides and Motion Pictures.* Grinnell, Iowa: Preservation Publishing Company, 1993. (Information and chapters from the book can also be downloaded at www.wilhelm-research.com.)

CHAPTER FOUR

Selling the Goods

Collier, Marsha. *eBay for Dummies.* 3rd edition. San Mateo, CA: IDG Books, 2002.

Collier, Marsha. *Starting an eBay Business for Dummies.* San Mateo, CA: IDG Books, 2001.

Pedigo, Cathy and Sonia Weiss. *The Pocket Idiot's Guide to Garage and Yard Sales.* Indianapolis: Alpha-Penguin Publishers, 2003.

Schmeltz, Les R. *The Backyard Money Machine: How to Organize and Operate a Successful Garage Sale.* Silver Streak Publishing, 1993.

Sinclair, Joseph T. *eBay the Smart Way: Selling, Buying and Profiting on the Web's #1 Auction Site. 2nd edition.* New York: American Management Association, 2000.

To learn more:

www.ConsignmentShops.com

www.YardSaleQueen.com

For selling books on-line:

www.alibris.com
This is a website for selling large collections of 500 books or more.

www.amazon.com
On this website you can sell individual books.

www.elephantbooks.com
This is a website for selling quality used, antiquarian, and scholarly books, as well as academic collections.

www.ecampus.com
This is a website for selling used textbooks.

www.powells.com
On this website, you can get information about selling books to the company, which will then sell them in their stores in Oregon or on-line.

www.textbookx.com
This is a website for selling used textbooks.

www.tomfolio.com
This is a website for selling used, rare, and collectible books, ephemera, and periodicals.

For information on collectibles:

www.Kovels.com

www.Curioscape.com

CHAPTER FIVE

Getting Rid of the Rest

For Recycling:

Earth 911
www.earth911.org
This website has an excellent list of resources for recycling and reuse centers organized by item and by state.

U.S. Environmental Protection Agency
Call (800) CLEANUP to locate local solid-waste agencies
www.epa.gov/opp00001/regulating/disposal.htm
The EPA's website gives general guidelines for the safe disposal of toxic waste and, to help locate state and local agencies, has a list of agencies and associations with telephone numbers and website addresses.

CHAPTER SIX

Lessons Learned

Lockwood, Georgene. *The Complete Idiot's Guide to Organizing Your Life.* 3rd edition. Indianapolis: Alpha-Penguin Publishers, 2002.

Luhrs, Janet. *The Simple Living Guide: A Sourcebook for Less Stressful, More Joyful Living.* New York: Broadway Books, 1997.

Morgenstern, Julie. *Organizing from the Inside Out.* New York: Owl Books, 1998.

Passoff, Michele. *Lighten Up! Free Yourself from Clutter.* New York: HarperCollins, 1998.

Peterson, Pipi Campbell. *Ready, Set, Organize: Get Your Stuff Together.* Indianapolis: Jist Publishing, 2002.

Schecter, Harriet. *Let Go of Clutter.* New York: McGraw Hill, 2000.

Schofield, Deniece. *Confessions of an Organized Homemaker: The Secrets of Uncluttering Your Home and Taking Control of Your Life.* Cincinnati: Betterway Publications, 1994.

Smallin, Donna. *Organizing Plain and Simple.* North Adams, MA: Storey Publishing, 2002.

Organizations

Professional, Trade, Consumer, and Support Groups

Appraisers

American Society of Appraisers (ASA)
555 Herndon Parkway, Suite 125
Herdon, VA 20170
Tel: (703) 478-2228
www.appraisers.org
This organization founded the Appraisal Foundation, which has issued the Uniform Standards of Professional Appraisal Practice(USPAP).

The Appraisal Foundation
1029 Vermont Avenue, N.W.,
Suite 900
Washington, D.C. 20005-3517
Tel: (202) 347-7722
www.appraisalfoundation.org
This organization has issued the Uniform Standards of Professional Appraisal Practice (USPAP).

Appraisers Association of America, Inc. (AAA)
386 Park Avenue
New York, NY 10016
Tel: (212) 889-5503
E-mail: aaa1@rcn.com
www.appraisersassoc.org
This is the oldest professional association of appraisers of personal property and the recognized authority for setting appraisal standards, legal issues, and regulation of the appraisal profession. The website has a database of members that can be searched by location and by specialty.

Association of Online Appraisers (AOA)
www.aoaonline.org
(AOA) is a registered not-for-profit international association for personal property appraisers who offer on-line written appraisal reports.

International Society of Appraisers (ISA)
1131 S.W. 7th Street, Suite 105
Renton, WA 98055
Tel: (206) 241-0359
Fax: (206) 241-0439
E-mail: isahq@isa-appraisers.org
www.isa-appraisers.org

Auctioneers

National Auctioneers Association
www.auctioneers.org
This website explains how to find an auctioneer, has a professional code of ethics, and provides lists of state and regional auctioneer associations.

Caregivers

Children of Aging Parents (CAPS)
1609 Woodbourne Road, Suite 302A
Levittown, PA 19057
Tel: (800) 227-7294
www.caps4caregivers.org
CAPS is a nonprofit organization that assists caregivers of the elderly or chronically ill with information, referrals, and support.

National Family Caregivers Association
10400 Connecticut Avenue, #500
Kensington, MD 20895
Tel: (800) 896-3650
E-mail: info@nfcacares.org
www.nfcares.org
The NFCA website lists publications and other resources for family caregivers.

Clutterers

Clutterers Anonymous (CLA)
P.O. Box 91413
Los Angeles, CA 90009-1413
www.clutterersanonymous.net
Provides information about local support group meetings, and seeks to help individuals who wish to minimize clutter in their lives.

Conservators

American Institute for the Conservation of Historic and Artistic Works (AIC)
1717 K Street N.W., Suite 200
Washington, D.C. 20006
Tel: (202) 452-9545
The website offers fact sheets with basic information about preserving various types of family treasures (from the home page, click on "Caring for Your Treasures").
It also features a guide that will help you locate conservators by specialty and area. (Click on "Selecting a Conservator.")
E-mail: info@aic-faic.org
http://aic.stanford.edu

Financial Planners/Advisors

Certified Financial Planner Board of Standards
Tel: (888) 237-6275
www.cfp-board.org
This website has a list of financial planners who are currently authorized by the CFP Board.

National Association of Personal Financial Advisors (NAPFA)
3250 North Arlington Heights Road, Suite 109
Arlington Heights, IL 60004
Tel: (800) 366-2732
www.napfa.org
NAPFA is the largest organization of financial planners. The website has a list of members.

Housing for the Elderly

American Association of Housing Services for the Aging (AAHSA)
2519 Connecticut Avenue, N.W.
Washington, D.C. 20008
Tel: (202) 783-2242
Fax: (202) 783-2255
E-mail: info@aahsa.org
www.aahsa.org

Lawyers for the Elderly

National Academy of Elder Law Attorneys, Inc.
1604 North Country Club Road
Tucson, AZ 85716
Tel: (520) 881-4005
Fax: (520) 325-7925
www.naela.com
This is a nonprofit association that assists lawyers, bar organizations, and others who work with older clients and their families.

Movers

American Moving and Storage Association
1611 Duke Street
Alexandria, VA 22314
Tel: (703) 683-7410
Fax: (703) 683-7527
E-mail: info@moving.org
www.moving.org
This association offers helpful consumer tips and other information regarding moving and storage.

Organizers

National Association of Professional Organizers (NAPO)
35 Technology Parkway, Suite 150
Norcross, GA 30092
www.napo.net
The website will help you find a professional organizer in your area.

Preservation and Local History

American Association for State and Local History (AASLH)
1717 Church Street
Nashville, TN 37203-2991
Tel: (615) 320-3203
E-mail: history@aaslh.org
www.aaslh.org

Preservation Directory.com
1507 S.W. 17th Avenue
Portland, OR 97201
Tel: (503) 223-4939
preservationdirectory@comcast.net
www.preservationdirectory.com
This on-line resource seeks to foster the preservation of cultural resources by facilitating communication among preservationists, historical societies, and the general public.

Retired Persons

American Association of Retired Persons (AARP)
601 E Street, N.W.
Washington, D.C. 20049
Tel: (800) 424-3410
www.aarp.org
Modern Maturity and *My Generation* have been merged into one publication, now called *AARP The Magazine*. The current issue can be accessed on-line.

Storage

Self-Storage Association
6506 Loisdale Road, Suite 315
Springfield, VA 22150
Tel: (703) 921-9123
E-mail: ssa@selfstorage.org
www.selfstorage.org
Helpful consumer information regarding self-storage units, and also some tips on moving: click on "Library," then "General Information."

Unclaimed Property

National Association of Unclaimed Property Administrators
www.unclaimed.org
This site was developed by state unclaimed-property experts to assist, free of charge, in efforts to search for funds that may belong to you or your relatives.

Suppliers of Archival Materials

The following suppliers offer archival storage materials and conservation supplies. Some of the websites also feature helpful information about proper storage conditions for various materials and other basic conservation information helpful to amateurs.

Conservation Resources International
8000-H Forbes Place
Springfield, VA 22151
Tel: (800) 634-6932
Fax: (703) 321-7730

Gaylord
P.O. Box 4901
Syracuse, NY 13221-4901
Tel: (800) 448-6160 (to order) or
(800) 634-6307 (customer service)
www.gaylord.com
Free pamphlets on preservation are available on request. Detailed information about proper care and storage for various materials is also available on their website.

Metal Edge, Inc.
6340 Bandini Blvd.
Commerce, CA 90040
Tel: 1(800) 862-2228
www.metaledgeinc.com

University Products, Inc.
517 Main Street
P.O. Box 101
Holyoke, MA 01041-0101
Tel: (800) 628-1912
www.universityproducts.com
The website offers a glossary of conservation terms.

Donation and Recycling Directory

National Charities

Goodwill
www.goodwill.org

Salvation Army
www.salvationarmy.org
To schedule a pick-up, call
1(800) 95-TRUCK.

Big Brothers Big Sisters of America
Tel: (215) 567-7000
www.bbbsa.org

Association of Junior Leagues International
Tel: (212) 951-8300
www.ajli.org

YWCA
Tel: (212) 273-7800
www.ywca.org

The Society of St. Vincent de Paul
This organization has offices in many cities and will pick up household items. Look them up in the white pages of the telephone book to locate the nearest facility.

Batteries, Rechargeable

Rechargeable Battery Recycling Corporation
www.rbrc.org
This site has a directory of places to drop off rechargeable batteries, which are recycled into new products.

Books

Books for America
2800 Quebec Street N.W.,
Suite 744
Washington, D.C. 20008
Tel: (202) 364-9737
E-mail: info@booksforamerica.org
www.booksforamerica.org
This organization accepts books (including encyclopedia sets), movies (VHS and DVD), music and instructional CDs, and video games and donates them to youth centers, women's shelters, hospices, and Veterans Administration hospitals. They have drop-off sites in the Washington, D.C. area, or items can be mailed via US Postal Service book rate.

Books for Africa
254 East 4th Street
St. Paul, MN 55101
Tel: (651) 602-9844
www.booksforafrica.org
This organization accepts textbooks from primary school through college level in all subjects except American history and civics, and foreign languages. Accepts *National Geographic* magazines from 1985 to the present. Especially needed: science and math books, college texts, and dictionaries.

The Book Thing of Baltimore, Inc.
2637 St. Paul Street
Baltimore, MD 21218
or
P.O. Box 2197
Baltimore, MD 21203
www.bookthing.org
This used bookstore gives away
books. Its mission is to put unwanted
books into the hands of those who
want them. It accepts donations of
books in person or mailed to one of
the addresses above.

BookCrossing
www.BookCrossing.com
This website calls itself a global
book club; it is attempting to
make the whole world a library.
One registers a book, receives a
label, and leaves book and label
in a public place.

Reach Out and Read (ROR)
www.reachoutandread.org
ROR promotes child literacy by
giving books to children at doctor's
visits. ROR will accept gently
used children's books; check the
website for guidelines and locations
in your area.

Cars

Kelley Blue Book
www.kbb.com

Edmunds
www.Edmunds.com

Both of these sources have a work-
sheet to determine the fair market
value of a car.

Cell Phones

Verizon's HopeLine Cell Phone Program
c/o ReCellular Inc.
2555 Bishop Circle West
Dexter, MI 48130
www.verizonwireless.com/hopeline
Donations are accepted at some
stores.

The Wireless Foundation / Call to Protect Program
Call to Protect
2555 Bishop Circle West
Dexter, MI 48130
Tel: (888) 901-SAFE
www.wirelessfoundation.org/Callto
Protect/index.cfm
Provides phones to victims of
domestic violence.

Charitable Recycling
www.charitablerecycling.com
A national program that accepts
donations of old cell phones by
mail and sends refurbished phones
to emerging countries as well as
within the U.S. Go to the website for
a shipping label.

Clothing

WOMEN'S CLOTHING

Dress for Success
Tel: (212) 545-3769 x 1
This is a local organization in New
York City that accepts women's pro-
fessional atire.

The Women's Alliance
www.thewomensalliance.org

A national organization of independent, community-based members who provide low-income women with professional attire. The website provides links to local organizations.

Career Gear
Tel: (212) 577-6190
www.careergear.org
This nonprofit organization provides clothing for interviews. It accepts clean, used, contemporary business clothing and new shoes.

Operation School Bell
Tel: (877) OSB-KIDS (672-5437)

Nike Reuse-A-Shoe
Nike Recycling Center
c/o Reuse-A-Show
26755 SW 95th Avenue
Wilsonville, OR 97070
Tel: (800) 352-NIKE
www.nikebiz.com
In this recycling program, worn-out athletic shoes are collected, ground up, and turned into athletic surfaces for kids to play on.
(Click on "Responsibility," then on "Reuse-a-Shoe.")

The Glass Slipper Project
c/o Midway Moving and Storage
2727 West Chicago Avenue
Chicago, IL 60622
www.glassslipperproject.org

Dress and accessory donations can be shipped by UPS or Federal Express. The website has a list of similar programs in other cities not associated with the Glass Slipper Project.

The Cinderella Project
www.thecinderellaproject.com
This website has lists of affiliated projects in various cities in Canada.

Some cities have their own websites:

Fairygodmotherproject@yahoo.com
(Boston)

www.fairygodmothersinc.org
(Philadelphia)

www.princessproject.org
(San Francisco)

Computers

Major manufacturers like IBM, Gateway, Hewlett-Packard, and Dell have programs for recycling unwanted hardware. Check the manufacturers' websites for the details of each program.

Computers for Children
237 Main Street,
Suite 400
Buffalo, NY 14203
Tel: (716) 843.8880
Fax: (716) 843.8883
E-mail: cfc@computersforchildren.com
www.computersforchildren.com
This organization upgrades personal computers and puts them into public schools.

Computers for Schools Organization
3642 North Springfield Avenue
Chicago, IL 60618
Tel: (800) 939-6000
www.pcsforschools.org
This website has a list by state
of places to donate computers
for refurbishing and donatation
to schools.

East West Education Development Foundation
55 Temple Place
Boston, MA 02111 (for mail)
582 East Street
Boston, MA 02210 (for shipments)
Tel: (617) 542-1234
Fax: (617) 542-3333
E-mail: Alex@donate.org
(To fax yourself information, call
(617) 542-2345, ask for ext. 101,
and give your fax number)
www.nonprofits.org/gallery/alpha/east
This nonprofit organization
recycles computer equipment
to educational and charitable
organizations in the U.S. and
in developing countries. It accepts
everything as-is, and not just the
latest generation.

PEP National Directory of Computer Recycling Programs
www.microweb.com/pepsite/Recycle/
recycle_index.html
[or www.microweb.com/pepsite and
click on Computer Recycling]
PEP (for Parents, Educators, and
Publishers of software) provides a list
of state, national, and international
agencies that facilitate donations of
used computer hardware to schools
and community groups.

www.Recycles.org
At this website, you can place an
offer to donate your equipment,
outdated as well as current, to the
Nonprofit Computer Recycling &
Reuse Network.

Share the Technology Project
www.sharetechnology.org/donate.html
This website provides a way for
donors and potential recipients
to connect, but encourages local
donations whenever possible to
avoid wasting energy by shipping
heavy computer equipment long dis-
tances. It has a computer donation
database with lists of requests from
schools, nonprofit organizations, and
people with disabilities. Also provides
free, postage-paid collection boxes
for used ink-jet and laser cartridges
and cellphones (recycle@sharetech-
nology.org).

World Computer Exchange (WCE)
936 Nantasket Avenue
Hull, MA 02045
Tel: (781) 925-3078
Fax: (509) 752-9186
www.worldcomputerexchange.org
WCE accepts donations of individual
Power Macs and Pentium PCs
(both tabletop and laptop) and/or
monitors in working condition,
shipped to the address above.

Eyeglasses

Lions Recycle for Sight
Lions Clubs International
Tel: (630) 571-5466
www.lionsclubs.org
This website has instructions for
donating eyeglasses.

LensCrafters
Tel: (800) 522-LENS
www.lenscrafters.com
You can bring glasses to any local
LensCrafters store.

New Eyes for the Needy, Inc.
549 Millburn Avenue
P.O. Box 332
Short Hills, NJ 07078
Tel: (973) 376-4903
www.PearleVision.com
You can bring glasses and sunglasses,
prescription or nonprescription, to
any Pearle Vision store.

Global Eye Care, Inc.
3013 Grand Concourse
New York, NY 10468
Tel: (718) 733-5730
www.Globaleyecare.org
This organization accepts used eyeglasses and sends them to developing
countries.

Food

America's Second Harvest
116 S. Michigan Avenue, #4
Chicago, IL 60603
Tel: (800) 771-2303
www.secondharvest.org
This is the largest domestic hunger
relief organization with a national
network of 189 food banks.

Gym Equipment

Operation Fit Kids
Tel: (800) 825-3636 x707
www.operationfitkids.org
This organization accepts new or
used equipment.

Hearing Aids

Hear Now
6700 Washington Avenue South
Eden Prairie, MN 55344
Tel: (800) 648-HEAR
You can send used hearing aids in a
padded envelope to the address above.

Letters

The Legacy Project
P.O. Box 53250
Washington, D.C. 20009
E-mail: warlettersproject@aol.com
www.warletters.com
This is a national, all-volunteer
effort to honor and remember those
who have served this nation in
wartime. It seeks out and saves letters
written to or received by members
of the armed forces, and donates
them to museums, archives, libraries,
or historical societies, in the interest
of preserving our history.

Medical Equipment

The first two organizations accept
medical equipment, but not medicine,
to send to developing countries.

MediSend International
6116 North Central Expressway,
Suite 305
Dallas, TX 75206
www.medisend.rog

The American Medical Resources Foundation
Tel: (508) 580-3301
Fax: (508) 580-3306
www.amrf.com

The National Multiple Sclerosis Society
www.nationalmssociety.org
Accepts medical equipment and loans it to those in need.

Musical Instruments

Save the Music
5436 Harvest Run Druve
San Diego, CA 92130-4878
Tel: (866) 968-7999
www.savethemusic.com
This site's "Instrument Xchange" facilitates the donation or exchange of used musical instruments.

Recycling

Earth 911
www.earth911.org
This website has an excellent list of resources for recycling and reuse centers organized by item and by state.

Toxic-Waste Disposal

U.S. Environmental Protection Agency
Call (800) CLEANUP to locate local solid-waste agencies
www.epa.gov/opp00001/regulating/disposal.htm
The EPA's website gives general guidelines for the safe disposal of toxic waste and, to help locate state and local agencies, has a list of agencies and associations with telephone numbers and website addresses.

A Checklist of Questions to Ask

EMPTYING THE HOUSE IS A BIG job and it can be overwhelming, but with the right approach, enough time, and a little bit of luck, clearing out the family home can also be a positive experience. ● Here is a set of questions to ask at different stages of the process. This checklist of things to think about and discuss with your family may help you be reasonably sure you are ready to move on to each successive stage of the process. We hope this will help you proceed as smoothly as possible, and may prevent misunderstandings between family members, or hasty actions that are later regretted. ● You may want to photocopy these pages and give a set to everyone involved in the process, to help you work together in a spirit of mutual understanding and with general agreement on how to proceed.

First Things First

The best way to begin the process, before any items are removed from the house, or even verbally claimed, is to talk with everyone in the family about what is happening.

☐ Has everyone in the family been consulted, and informed, that we are about to start emptying the house?

☐ Have we made a family plan for how to go about this process? Has everyone agreed to it?

☐ Have we set a date when the process will begin? Is it clear to everyone who will be involved?

☐ Have we talked about how to handle any disagreements or disputes that may arise in the process?

☐ Have we dealt with any disagreements about any of the above as well as we can? If we are not all in agreement, do we at least have a consensus that the process should begin? (Note: Families who become deadlocked before they even begin will find some great ideas and information about how other families have dealt with this process at www.yellowpieplate.umn.edu.)

Sorting It Out

It's a daunting task to have to make decisions about each and every item in the house. The following questions may help you see the decisions you are making in a new light.

☐ Does the cost of shipping and/or storing an item (or items) make sense from an economic point of view? (Could I buy new items of the same or better quality for less than the cost of packing and shipping the old ones?)

☐ If I throw this out in a fit of exhaustion or annoyance, will my children or grandchildren regret it? Will my brother (or my uncle) resent my doing so?

☐ Am I throwing this out because I really don't want it, or because I don't know what to do with it?

☐ Will I use this item? Do I have an emotional attachment to it? Or, am I holding on to it simply because it belonged to my parents?

☐ Am I the caretaker for all of our family's stuff? Can someone else in the family share this role?

☐ Can a decision about a disputed item, or issue within the family, wait? Why does it have to be decided right now? Can it wait an hour? a day? a week?

Saving Precious Memories

Special things that have been passed down in the family, whether they are photographs, furniture, china, silver, or fabric, require and deserve special treatment to ensure that they will remain in good condition for future generations.

☐ Have we set aside and found a safe place for anything that is important to our family?

☐ Have we made sure that fragile items are properly packed or stored?

☐ If we are putting things into storage, have the boxes or envelopes been clearly marked? Is the storage space appropriate and safe for the materials we are storing?

☐ Have family treasures that need to be repaired or restored been placed in temporarily in a safe place until we can get them to a professional for treatment? Has someone in the family agreed to take on the responsibility for following through with this?

Selling the Goods

There are many different ways to sell the things that no one in your family wants—whether it's for a little money at a yard sale, or for a lot at an auction. Make sure all interested parties are in agreement before anything is put up for sale.

☐ Have all involved persons given their consent to sell the objects that are about to go on sale?

☐ If you are holding an estate sale or auction, have things that are not for sale been set aside in a safe place? Has it been made clear to whoever will be operating the sale that these things are not to be sold?

☐ If there is to be an auction or estate sale, has someone in the family carefully reviewed the contract, and asked any questions that family members may have?

☐ Have we given special consideration to any collections in the house? Has someone done at least a bit of research to make sure that if a collection or collectible items are sold, they are sold in an appropriate way?

Getting Rid of the Rest

As the pace picks up, it's easy to get carried away and start toss-ing things quickly and carelessly. Taking the time to check and even double-check things that are leaving the house forever, whether they are headed for charity or the trash, is a good idea.

☐ Has everyone involved in the process given their consent to getting rid of the things that are being given away, donated, or thrown away?

☐ Has someone carefully checked through everything that is going out of the house to make sure nothing important is lost?

☐ Do we, or does the estate, need a tax receipt for things that are being donated? If so, have we made arrangements to get itemized receipts?

☐ Has someone checked local safety and environmental regulations before throwing out toxic waste?

Lessons Learned

When you find yourself confronted with the challenge of emptying the contents of an entire house, the temptation to rush the process is strong. Take a look at these common regrets that people who have been through the process have had, and try to avoid them.

- [ ] Threw out, or gave away, things I now wish I had.

- [ ] Sold something valuable for too little.

- [ ] Gave away items my siblings later wanted.

- [ ] Broke or lost valuable or special things in the process of emptying the house.

- [ ] Stored items I ended up throwing out or giving away, for too long.

- [ ] Kept things not because I really wanted or needed them, but just because they belonged to my parents.

Index

Acknowledgments

WRITING A BOOK IS ALWAYS a collaborative effort and many people were helpful to us as we gathered the information and stories we have included here. For taking the time to talk with us and to answer our many questions about their respective areas of expertise thoroughly and patiently, we are grateful to Kathy Bartholow, Kristine Fladeboe Duininck, Linda Edquist, Helaine Fendelman, George Hulstrand, Mona Nelson, Dr. Marlene Stum, and Dr. Norma Thomas.

Others have helped us in a more general way over a period of months or years: thanks to Andrea DiNoto, Anne Kostick, Darlene Schroeder, and Sally Steenland, for providing invaluable professional guidance, friendship, enthusiasm, and all-round support. And many thanks also to our families, for being there for us, and—given the personal nature of some of what is covered in this book—for not asking us too much about what we were planning to say.

Marisa Bulzone, our editor, believed in the value of a book like this one, and trusted us to be the ones to write it. Her enthusiasm for and instant understanding of the topic set the stage for an easy and productive collaboration; she provided us with skillful, professional, and sensitive guidance at key moments in the process, and allowed us to figure out the details as we saw fit. Thanks to Susi Oberhelman for the elegance of her design and the depth of her patience, and to David McGrievey for his wonderful illustrations. Thanks also to Trudi Bartow for her editorial assistance and to the publicity and marketing team at STC for championing the book.

Of course this book would not have been possible without the enthusiastic support and participation of the many people we interviewed who shared their memories and some of their best ideas with us. Because of the sensitive and highly personal nature of some of the material we gathered in these interviews, and in order to protect the privacy and confidentiality of all concerned, we have chosen not to thank any of these individuals by name. But they know who they are; and we are very grateful to everyone who took the time to share their feelings, thoughts, and ideas with us, and in turn with the readers of our book.

L I N D A   H E T Z E R is the author of *Rainy Days and Saturdays* (Workman), *50 Fabulous Parties for Kids* (Crown Publishing), *The Simple Art of Napkin Folding* (Hearst Books/HarperCollins), and *Illustrated Crafts for Beginners* (Raintree Books). She is a freelance writer and editorial consultant whose clients include Artisan Publishing, Sunset Books, Reader's Digest, Time-Life Books, Hearst Books, Andrews & McMeel, and the National Audubon Society. She lives in New York with her husband, Michael Ginsburg, a photographer, and their two children.

J A N E T   H U L S T R A N D is a writer and editor who has had a substantial editorial role in the writing of many books and articles on a wide variety of topics. She is the creator of "Paris Through the Eyes of Travelers," and "Hawaii: Island Paradise Where East and West Meet," literature courses she teaches through the Hunter College Study Abroad program. She was intimately involved in the emptying of one house and, now that this book exists, can hardly wait to empty the next. She lives in Washington D.C. with her husband, Stephen Rueckert, a sculptor, and their two children.